ROCKLAND COUNTY
NEW YORK
IN THE 1790s

"View of Tappan, or Orange Town, taken 28th Septr. 1778 and finished 15th
June 1780 on board the Littledale Transport on the Passage from Charles
Town to New York. A.R.," sepia drawing by Archibald Robertson.
Spencer Collection, The New York Public Library.

ROCKLAND COUNTY
NEW YORK
IN THE 1790s

Jacquetta M. Haley

The Historical Society of Rockland County
New City, New York
1997

Library Research Associates, Inc.
474 Dunderberg Road
Monroe, New York 10950

Edited by Marianne B. Leese

Library of Congress Cataloging-in-Publication Data:
Haley, Jacquetta M. (1948-   )
    Rockland County, New York in the 1790s /
    by Jacquetta M. Haley.
        156p.
    Includes index.
    ISBN:0-911183-42-6
    1. Rockland County (N.Y.)—History. I. Title.
F127.R6H35   1997
974.7'2803—dc20   96-46190
                                                        CIP

~

Table of Contents

Rockland County Bicentennial

1798-1998

Welcoming People for 200 Years

☙

Foreword

The occasion for this book is the 200th anniversary of the establishment of Rockland as a county. To reflect the wide-ranging diversity of the people of the county, the Rockland County Bicentennial Commission chose as its motto, "Welcoming People for 200 Years." Ms. Haley's delightful and readable study acquaints Rocklanders with their county's history and inspires further research into its unique heritage.

Rockland is the smallest county in the State of New York, outside the five boroughs of New York City. The rocky nature of the soil and the great formations of rock that rise as cliffs above the shore of the Hudson River and thrust up through the interior mountainsides, understandably gave Rockland County its name.

Until the 1950s it was a county with an agricultural and small business tradition. Contact with neighboring counties and with the great city to the south was limited to trading goods and farm produce and to a modest tourist business. The opening of the Tappan Zee Bridge and completion of the New York State Thruway and the Palisades Interstate Parkway changed Rockland into a vibrant and fast-growing suburb of New York City.

Before this land became Rockland County, the André-Arnold drama was played out here and the pivotal battle of Stony Point was fought here. Today more than a hundred homes and buildings designated as landmarks dot the county. Among the existing examples of Rockland's heritage are George Washington's headquarters in Tappan, the Jacob Blauvelt House in New City, and the Stony Point Battlefield and Lighthouse.

When the English established counties in their New York territory, the area that is now Rockland was part of Orange County. The Ramapo Mountains provided a natural barrier that divided Orange County and gave rise to the Rockland section being known as the land "South of the Mountains." The location of the county seat in the southernmost part proved a hardship for citizens "North of the Mountains." As a result, a long, drawn-out movement began to establish a separate county.

This is the story of Rockland's road to political independence. But even more importantly, it is about what life was like in the county in the late 18th and early 19th centuries. The isolating effect of mountainous terrain and the absence of navigable inland waterways is revealed, and we discover how people farmed, traveled, and lived their lives.

Thomas F. X. Casey
Rockland County Historian and
President, Rockland County
Bicentennial Commission.

Chapter 1

The Creation
of
Rockland County

In February 1798 the residents of Orange County, South of the Mountains, finished something that had begun a quarter of a century earlier, the establishment of their own separate county, Rockland County.[1] Since 1683 the Rockland area had been the southernmost part of Orange County. Now it would exist on its own.

Some might say that the drive to create a distinct identity for Rockland had begun as far back as 1727, when the inhabitants North of the Mountains (modern Orange County) successfully argued that it was too difficult to attend county court in Tappan because of the nearly impassable mountain range that split the county in two. They asked for, and got, sessions of the county court that alternated between Tappan and Goshen (1727). Then, in 1737, the General Assembly of New York authorized the building of a second county courthouse and gaol in Goshen. County business would alternate between the two county centers, giving residents on either side of the mountains better access to the courts for county business and other legal matters.

---

(1) "An Act for dividing the county of Orange," February 23, 1798, Chap. 16, 21st Sess., *Laws of the State of New York*, vol. 4 (Albany, N.Y.: Weed, Parsons, & Co. Printers, 1887), pp. 156-158.

The 1798 split of old Orange County into Rockland County (South of the Mountains) and Orange County (North of the Mountains)[2] culminated over half a century of political maneuvers that legally acknowledged what geography had already made evident. In an era that lacked transportation capabilities beyond foot, horse, or sail, the Ramapo Mountains successfully limited travel and communication between the two halves of old Orange County. As the 18th century came to a close, it became evident that two separate populations with different interests had emerged. The formation of two counties allowed the two areas to protect their own interests and proceed into the 19th century under their own leadership.

Initially southern Orange, the area that would become Rockland County, was the most dynamic part of old Orange County. Settlers arrived in the Tappan and Haverstraw areas in the 1680s. However, by 1798 the once dominant area of southern Orange had become the less vigorous partner. The lands north and west of the Ramapos had grown much more rapidly than the smaller triangle that became Rockland County. This northern and western population outnumbered the future Rocklanders nearly three to one. Their lands were more suited to farming, and they had readier access to roads.

The Movement to Split Orange County

The provincial legislature recognized the inherent geographic difficulties encountered by the residents of old Orange County by permitting the establishment of a separate court district in Goshen in 1727 and then ordering the construction of a second courthouse and gaol in 1737. The actual movement to split the county, however, began in February 1772. At that time John De Noyelles, one of the representatives of old Orange County in the General Assembly of New York, introduced a bill to have the assemblymen from Orange County represent the two distinct areas separated by the mountains. At that time the two Orange County men represented the county at large. De Noyelles wanted one to represent the specific interests of the inhabitants North of the Mountains; the other, the interests of the inhabitants South of the Mountains.

---

(2)   The new Orange County would include several towns that had formerly belonged in
       southern Ulster County.

Mr. De Noyelles, a resident of the Haverstraw Precinct, had the support of many residents South of the Mountains, but far less support among those to the north.[3] A petition, "signed by a number of people of Haverstraw Precinct & some few of Tappan," reiterated local support for the De Noyelles bill when it requested

> that the Freeholders of each Side of the Mountain in your County shoud [sic] respectively chuse a Representative for the said County without allowing the People on the South Side to vote for the one on the North Side or those on the North Side to vote for the Member to be elected on the South Side.[4]

Opposition to Dividing the County

Opposition to the proposed change in the method of selecting Orange County's assemblymen was most obvious outside Orange County. New York State's future governor, George Clinton, then the representative from Ulster County, felt strongly that the proposed alteration to representation in Orange County should be defeated. He wrote to Henry Wisner, a prominent Goshen resident, suggesting that Wisner circulate an opposing petition among the people North of the Mountains. Clinton further suggested that Wisner have copies of the opposing petitions sent to both the governor and the Provincial Council. In this way, if by chance the General Assembly passed the De Noyelles bill, the governor and the council would already be prepared to kill further action. Clinton even offered to write the petition himself but requested that his part in the preparation and circulation of the petition be kept quiet.[5]

Either because of Clinton's behind-the-scenes manipulations or because of a general dislike of any move to alter the existing system of representation, De Noyelles's proposal was defeated, 11 to 9. As would be expected, De Noyelles voted for his proposal, while Samuel Gale of

(3)   De Noyelles introduced his bill February 4, 1772, *Journal of the Votes and Proceedings of the General Assembly of the Colony of New York, January to March 1772*, p. 61. See George H. Budke, "The Formation of the County of Rockland, New York in 1798," *The Rockland Record*, II (1931 & 1932), pp. 61-64 for a detailed discussion of the drive to create a separate county.

(4)   George Clinton to Henry Wisner, February 6, 1772, Collections of the Goshen Public Library and Historical Society, Goshen, New York.

(5)   Clinton to Henry Wisner, February 6, 1772.

Goshen, the other representative from Orange County, voted against the measure.[6]

De Noyelles did not give up on his drive to achieve separate representation for the area South of the Mountains. In January 1774 he introduced a bill that would have created a new County of Lancaster out of southern Orange County. This proposal brought a barrage of petitions from residents on both sides of the mountains, some in favor, and many opposed.[7] In general, residents on the north side opposed the division of the county while those to the south were divided. Petitions from northern Orange against the creation of a new county bore 720 signatures while those against it from the south had 311 names. The petitions favoring such a split of the county bore the signatures of 354 southern residents. The bill, when brought to a final vote in February, was defeated 14 to 12. De Noyelles obviously voted in favor of the new county. Gale voted against it.[8]

The opposition to the creation of a new county had rallied around an anonymous pamphlet published in 1774: *The Case of the County of Orange.* Here the attempt to split Orange County was compared to the creation of "rotten Boroughs" in England. The author pointed out that the proposed southern county would be significantly smaller than any other area currently represented in the colonial assembly. This seemed especially unreasonable as there had just been a significant decrease in the southern population because of the transfer of several residents to New Jersey's jurisdiction in 1771 (due to the settlement of the boundary dispute between New York and New Jersey). In the 1769 provincial elections, the area South of the Mountains had not been able to field even 400 voters. The 1771 changes brought the number of freeholders in southern Orange eligible to vote for provincial representatives down to only 260.

The pamphlet further pointed out that the southern precinct had a very small tax base. South of the Mountains was assessed for only £1,420, while the assessment for the residents North of the Mountains was £2,230. The pamphleteer denied any wish to "impeach the Integrity, or to represent, as sinister, the Views of any one Member of the House," but he pointed out that the proposal "runs so counter to all

(6)   *Journal of Votes and Proceedings*, 1772, p. 61.

(7)   The petitions themselves do not survive, although record of their submission to the General Assembly can be found in *Journal of Votes and Proceedings*, 1774, pp. 39, 64.

(8)   *Journal of Votes and Proceedings*, 1774, p. 64.

sound Reason and good Policy" that one could be tempted to call it "the spurious Offspring of sinister Design." The author of the pamphlet obviously believed that the creation of a new county with such a small population was actually an effort on the part of a few individuals to acquire an unseemly amount of power.[9]

Revival of Movement to Divide the County

The death of John De Noyelles in January 1775 and the eruption of the American Revolution pushed any thoughts about the division of Orange County out of the political arena for over a decade. When discussions began again in the late 1780s, the center of political and economic power in old Orange County had clearly shifted. It would be the residents North of the Mountains who now provided the impetus for the division of the county.

A 1787 petition to the state assembly began, "By reason of a very extensive and almost impassable range of mountains running across said county and near the center thereof," the petitioners were "put to numberless hardships and many heavy expenses in attending courts and transacting the other necessary business of the county."[10] The northern petitioners proposed the division of the county north and south of the mountains, with the addition of a strip of land in the southern part of Ulster County to the northern half of old Orange County. There is no record of how the petition was received, but the movement for division was once again in motion. This time, however, there were two significant differences.

First, the momentum for the division came from North of the Mountains rather than South of the Mountains. Second, the expansion of New York State into the western lands formerly held by the Iroquois Nation meant that several new counties, many with relatively small populations, had already been erected in other areas of the state. It would no longer be a case of a small portion of one of the old counties

(9)   *The Case of the County of Orange, with Observations, to shew the Injustice of the Division of that County into two; and the Perilous Consequences of splitting the Colony into such little dependent Districts, as will render them the Prey of Ambition, and the Instruments of Corruption,* typescript of original, Budke Collection, BC-32, The New York Public Library.

(10) "The petition of the inhabitants of the northern part of the County of Orange," January 10, 1787, in Budke, "The Formation of the County of Rockland, New York in 1798," *The Rockland Record,* II, pp. 63-64.

getting special treatment, as would have been true in 1772 and 1774. Instead, the division of old Orange County into two more easily administered counties would be just one of several similar divisions. Rockland County was one of 17 new counties erected between the end of the Revolution and the beginning of the 19th century.

Nothing came of the 1787 petition, but the residents North of the Mountains began a decade-long drive to resolve the problems caused by having their county seat located at New City, South of the Mountains. This was at least closer than the original county seat in Tappan, but the problem of accessibility had not been solved by the 1774 construction of a new county courthouse in New City. In some ways, New City was even more of a problem. Tappan had at least been readily accessible by river. New City could be reached only by road, and it was really in the middle of nowhere.

Sentiment for Division in Ulster County

Those Orange County citizens who wanted their county seat in Goshen began discussions with a group of residents in the Newburgh area of southern Ulster. These Ulster County residents had a problem similar to that of their Orange County neighbors. Just as the inhabitants of Orange County in Cornwall and the riverside communities had to travel nearly 30 miles south to enter their records in Tappan and later in New City, the inhabitants of Newburgh and surrounding communities had to travel nearly 30 miles north to Kingston with their official documents.

Representatives from northern Orange County and southern Ulster met in Ward's Bridge (modern Montgomery) on April 6, 1793 to discuss a possible union. They were unable to reach any definite agreement. The delegates from Goshen displayed only a lukewarm willingness to consider their inclusion in a new county that would include both the northern towns of Orange and the southern towns of Ulster. The Ulster delegates wanted the county court to alternate between Newburgh and Goshen. The Orange County delegates did not want to have another split court. A second convention, this time at Otterkill, took place in February 1794. Again, the delegates failed to agree on the erection of a new county. The location of the county seat was once again the sticking point. The delegates from Newburgh would accept union with the Orange County towns only if there was agreement that court proceedings would alternate between Goshen and

Newburgh. The Goshen delegates would not give this proposal their complete support since it meant a continued diminution of their own position as county seat. They already had a shared county seat in New City. A similar arrangement with Newburgh did not represent a great improvement.

Legislature Approves Division

Finally, in 1797, a third convention of delegates from northern Orange and southern Ulster met, this time in Little Britain. At this meeting General Wilkin and General Hopkins of Orange County and David Niven and Isaac Belknap, Sr., of Ulster came to terms. They agreed that the courts would meet alternately at Newburgh and Goshen. The convention ratified the agreement and a bill to divide Orange County in two was presented to the state legislature during the winter term of 1796-1797. Two bills were presented. One, "An Act for dividing the county of Orange," resulted in the creation of a separate county South of the Mountains, today's Rockland County. The second bill, "An Act for altering the bounds of the counties of Orange and Ulster," realigned the boundary between these two counties and established two court jurisdictions to meet the needs of Orange County as it was redrawn with the Ulster townships.[11]

Throughout this 1790s debate on the division of Orange County, the inhabitants South of the Mountains appear to have remained relatively silent. The discussion really revolved around resolving issues between Ulster and Orange rather than any debate on the separate identity of the southern third of old Orange County. By this time inhabitants North of the Mountains far outnumbered their counterparts to the south. Having suffered fewer depredations during the American Revolution, they enjoyed a much greater degree of prosperity than their more southern neighbors. They exhibited a different population mix. The overwhelming majority were of English extraction, while families of Dutch ancestry remained both numerous and prominent South of the Mountains.

The final establishment of Rockland County on February 23,

---

(11)   The above account of the movement to divide Orange County in the 1790s is taken from E.M. Ruttenber and L.H. Clark, comps., *History of Orange County, New York*, 2 vols. (1881; reprint ed., Interlaken, N.Y.: Heart of the Lakes Publishing, 1980), 1:27-29.

1798 ended a quarter century of debate on how the lands on the western shore of the Hudson River could be most easily administered. Geography had won out over man's artificial dividing lines. Rockland and Orange counties could now go their separate ways.

In Rockland County, geography probably has been the most significant factor influencing the development of the area. Its apparent inaccessibility, particularly when compared with the neighboring lands across the Hudson River, encouraged slow population growth and the continued isolation of many interior areas of the county throughout the 18th and 19th centuries. Eventually the introduction of new technologies in transportation and communication in the mid-19th and 20th centuries would begin to break down some of Rockland's remote, inaccessible image. By the last half of the 20th century it would resemble, in many ways, other nearby counties that had been transformed into suburbs of New York City at a much earlier date. However, the transformation took nearly 200 years. Rockland remained a remote, agricultural area with strong ties to its Dutch colonial ancestry long after its neighbors, especially those across the river in Westchester County or in northern New Jersey, had taken on a more suburban appearance.

The following pages describe that early Rockland of the 1790s. It was a Rockland dominated by geography. The ability, or inability, to move from one part of the county to another affected all aspects of life in the county. Thus a look at the early transportation system, the roads, the rivers, and their limitations, is critical to understanding life in Rockland at the end of the 18th century. Chapter 2, "The Geography of Rockland County, or You Can't Get There from Here," discusses these problems.

A second key factor affecting life in Rockland was agriculture. Farming was the economic base of Rockland and dictated just about all other activities. The fields had to be plowed, animals bred, the crops harvested, the food preserved and stored. Once these essentials had been taken care of, other ancillary interests could be considered, but as adjuncts to farming, not as replacements for it. Everyday life in Rockland rested on an understanding of the seasonal chores that had to be accomplished to ensure a successful harvest and a well-stocked larder for the cold winter months.   "Life in an Agricultural Community," chapter 3, examines this fundamental underpinning of life and death on the western banks of the Hudson River.

Lastly, life in Rockland meant people — the men and women who lived, worked, and died here. "The People of Rockland County," chapter 4, looks at all the inhabitants, rather than at a few prominent men. Using early census data, a general portrait of the different characters of Orangetown and Haverstraw emerges. They differed in terms of wealth, sex, race, age, and general ethnic mix. Rockland was not homogeneous. There were distinct differences among the four townships that made up Rockland at the end of the century. The population mix reflected those differences.

A Note on Place Names

Names, particularly in the 18th century, were not fixed for all time. They changed as spellings and pronunciations changed. They also changed to meet new needs. This is particularly apparent in some of the place names used in Rockland in the 18th century. The selection of the name "Rockland" for the county is something of a problem in itself. No one really knows why it was selected. The term has had a long association with southernmost Rockland. Its first recorded use was in 1714. At that time Captain John Corbett, the owner of the lands currently known as Palisades or Snedens Landing, referred to his property as "Rockland" in his last will and testament.[12] It was clearly an appropriate name for a county most obviously distinguished by the rocky Ramapo Mountains that generally gave it an inhospitable appearance. In addition, the rocky nature of the soil certainly made "Rockland" a fitting appellation for the area.

Several place names in Rockland have undergone changes over the last years. Some of the places that were familiar to Rocklanders in 1790 seem to have disappeared completely. In these pages, the late 18th-century names are generally used since these are the names that are used in the period references. The most notable differences occur in the use of the words Haverstraw and Hempstead. Originally "Haverstraw" referred to the small settlement in northern Rockland along the Hudson River. In 1719 the Precinct of Haverstraw, meaning all of Rockland north of Orangetown, was erected. This became the Town of Haverstraw in 1788. In 1791, the Town of Haverstraw was divided into the towns of Clarkstown, New Hempstead, and

(12)   Budke, "Formation of County of Rockland," p. 64.

Haverstraw. When late 18th-century documents referred to going to Haverstraw, they meant going to the hamlet of Haverstraw.

"Hempstead," as a place name, has undergone similar permutations. Hempstead was the name used for modern Ramapo Township beginning in 1797. Originally, the term "New Hempstead" arrived in Rockland with English colonists from Hempstead, Long Island, who settled the center of the county beginning around 1720. They settled in an area generally referred to as "Kakiat" but also referred to as New Hempstead, to distinguish it from Hempstead, Long Island. During the second half of the 18th century, Kakiat, New Hempstead, and Hempstead were all used to refer to the crossroads where the road from Suffern (then called New Antrim) to Haverstraw intersected with the road to New City. The term "Kakiat" will be used to refer to this crossroads area. The 1791 act that divided Haverstraw Township into three towns called the largest township New Hempstead (official state records show the name spelled as "New Hampstead" as do many locally recorded deeds and other legal documents). The "New" was quickly dropped from common usage so that Hempstead (Hampstead) became the official name by 1797. In 1829, the postal service forced Rockland to change the name of the township from Hempstead to Ramapo.

"Clarkstown" refers to both the township established in 1791 and the crossroads area now known as West Nyack. In the 1790s Clarkstown and New City were the principal population centers in the modern Township of Clarkstown.

Orangetown, as the oldest settled portion of Rockland, has kept most of its early place names. However, "Slote" refers to the area at the mouth of the Sparkill Creek, now known as Piermont.

The very idiomatic spelling used throughout the 18th century further complicates the issue of place names, particularly with regard to "Hempstead," "Hampstead," "Hempsted," and "Hampsted." Throughout this period no fixed spelling had been established. Each writer spelled phonetically as he or she saw fit. Modern spellings for place names are used here.

The map on page 25, "Principal Roads in Rockland County in the 1790s," gives both the preferred 18th-century place name and its 20th-century counterpart.

The Budke Collection

This work would not have been possible without the thorough, dedicated work of George H. Budke (1868-1948). Mr. Budke spent years diligently searching out and collecting materials relating to Rockland County's history and to the genealogies of its residents. His collection, located at the New York Public Library, is an invaluable resource for the historians of Rockland County. Microfilm copies of his collection (except for maps) are available at the New City Public Library. Print copies of part of the collection may be found at the New City Public Library as well as at other libraries within Rockland County.

"A View in Hudson's River of the Entrance of what is called the Topan Sea.
Sketch'd on the SPOT by his Excellency Governor Pownal,
Painted by Paul Sandby, Engraved by Peter Benazech." Circa 1761.
Collections of Historic Hudson Valley, Tarrytown, New York.

Chapter 2

๙

The Geography of Rockland County,

or

You Can't Get There from Here

About ten or twelve miles from New York, the western shore appears quite different from what it was before; it consists of steep mountains with perpendicular sides towards the river, and they are exactly like the steep sides of the mountains of Hall and Hunnebarg in West Gothland. Sometimes a rock projects like the salient angle of a bastion: the tops of these mountains are covered with oaks, and other wood; a number of stones of all sizes lay along the shore, having rolled down from the mountains.

These high and steep mountains continue for some English miles on the western shore; but on the eastern side the land is high, and sometimes diversified with hills and valleys, which are commonly covered with deciduous trees, amongst which there appears a farm now and then in a glade....

About twenty-two miles from New York, the high mountains which I have before mentioned left us, and made as it were a high ridge here from east to west quite across the country. This altered the face of the country on the western shore of the river: from mountainous, it be-

came interspersed with little vallies and round hillocks,
which were scarce inhabited at all; but the eastern shore
continued to afford us a delightful prospect.[1]

Peter Kalm's voyage up the Hudson in 1749 illustrates the principal
reason Rockland failed to attract large numbers of settlers
throughout the 18th century as well as in the 19th century. In an
era when the principal highways were rivers, Rockland County had
little to attract the casual visitor and even less to draw the potential
settler away from the more desirable lands on the east side of the
Hudson. The Hudson River was the highway into New York. Sail up
the Hudson, and then at Albany follow the Mohawk Valley into central
and western New York. Or, follow the valleys of the Hudson's smaller
tributaries into the interior. Viewed from a sloop in the middle of the
Hudson River, the land on the eastern shore, particularly Westchester
County, included visible farmsteads on rolling wooded hillsides. A
potential settler could visualize his future on a neat, prosperous
farmstead with an orchard, livestock grazing in the pastures, and fields
abundantly planted in wheat and corn.

The impression gained of Rockland from that same sloop was
far less favorable. While the eastern shore sloped down to the river
bank, with several small hamlets and lanes leading from the river
inland, the western shore was rocky with few access points for the
interior. It rose abruptly to a plateau several hundred feet above river
level. The few rivers and creeks that led inland, in particular the Spar
Kill (Sparkill Creek), offered only limited access to Rockland's interior.

Sloops could enter the Spar Kill at high tide, but only if they
carried a light load. Orangetown's earliest settlers had cut an artificial
channel, or ditch, through the meadow at the mouth of the creek. This
narrow channel, known as the "Slote," allowed vessels to sail a short
way up the Spar Kill to a dock. The small community around the dock
was Tappan Slote, or just Slote. Vessels could sail up to the dock if
they had little cargo. When loaded, the boat had to be pulled, by men,

---

(1)   Peter Kalm, *Travels into North America*, trans. John Reinhold Forster, introd. Ralph M.
Sargent (Barre, Mass.: The Imprint Society, 1972), June 10, 1749, pp. 316-317.

through the "Slote" to the dock and then back out into the Hudson. Tappan Slote, at modern Piermont, remained the major access point for goods, materials, and people coming to southern Rockland throughout the 18th century.[2] But it offered little inducement to the farmer looking for new lands to settle. Even by the time of Peter Kalm's visit, after nearly 65 years of settlement in Rockland, there was little in the way of human habitation to nullify the seemingly inhospitable nature of the landscape. The men and women who wanted good lands to farm with access to the major market in New York City seldom viewed the western shore of the Hudson River Valley with favorable eyes.

Those people who traveled by road were as unimpressed with Rockland County lands as those who sailed up the Hudson. Roads in 18th-century New York ran the gamut from relatively wide, well-maintained lanes suitable for wagons, carts, and horses to narrow, winding pathways that were suitable for foot, or possibly a single horse. The key factors in building and maintaining good roadways were a favorable geography and a population large enough to maintain the roads. Rockland's mountainous terrain, its lack of broad river or creek valleys winding into the interior, and its lack of a solid population base to build and then maintain the roads, all played a continuing role in restricting access to the county and inhibiting any rapid movement of population into the interior.

Land Transportation in 18th-Century New York

New York State built its system of roads on the framework established during the colonial years, beginning in the summer of 1703. At that time New York's colonial legislature first outlined the proposed development of roadways throughout its jurisdiction, including latter-day Rockland, with "An Act for the Laying out Regulateing Clearing and preserving Publick Comon highways thro'out this Colony."[3] This act established the initial system of King's Highways, or King's Roads, through New York Colony, identified existing roads as part of a

---

(2)   Rev. David Cole, D.D., ed., *History of Rockland County, New York* (1884; reprint ed., New City, N.Y.: The Historical Society of Rockland County, 1986), p. 220.
(3)   New York State, *The Colonial Laws of New York from the Year 1664 to the Revolution*, 5 vols. (Albany, N.Y.: James B. Lyon, State Printer, 1894), 1:532-538.

common highway network open to all, and set up the basic definition of what a road would be. Existing lanes and paths, and future lanes, linked local traffic to the King's Road, "and to Such Convenient Landing places in each respective Town and Village" as to allow "for the better & easier Transportacon [sic] of goods and the Commodious passing of Travellers." It was hoped that such a road system would promote and encourage commerce throughout the colony.

One of the first five public highways established in 1703 was the road from the southern border of Orange County to Albany and beyond to Schenectady. This was the King's Road, or Albany Road, the principal north-south route on the west side of the Hudson River. It was never as well traveled as its counterpart on the eastern shore. Unlike the Albany Post Road on the east side of the Hudson, it did not hug the shore but traveled inland through the Ramapo Mountains and then swung eastward to Newburgh and on north to Albany. This first King's Road had relatively little impact on travel through Rockland because it touched only the westernmost part of the county. Other roads, generally running north-south between the Hudson River on the east and the Ramapo Mountains on the west, became the principal internal land routes.

Based on the 1703 legislation, all these highways and public roads should have been four to six rods wide. A rod is 5½ yards, or 16½ feet. All existing roads were supposed to be widened to a minimum of four rods, while all new roads would be six rods wide. These widths really constituted a right of way rather than the actual width of the road surface. It was the ideal rather than the reality. The excessively rugged terrain in Orange and Dutchess counties led the colony's legislators to give special dispensations for their roads. Although "planned" future roadways were to meet the six-rod standard, Orange and Dutchess county were not required to clear or maintain any path or highway beyond what was necessary for "Horse and man only." This minimal requirement remained in effect until population growth and increased traffic within the counties called for wider roads more suited to wheeled traffic.

Road Maintenance

The 1703 legislation also created the position of road commissioner. These men, and there were several in each county, laid out the paths for all current and future roadways and undertook to see that those roadways were properly repaired and maintained once opened.

During the remaining years of colonial rule, the legislature passed periodic updates to this basic road legislation, usually expanding on the duties and responsibilities of local residents with regard to the road system. In 1708 the framework for all future roadwork and maintenance in New York was established. The inhabitants and free-holders who lived adjacent to and used each stretch of road became responsible for its clearance and maintenance. The road commission-ers could call upon each resident for six days a year of labor to repair the roads. That maintenance consisted of "cutting up the brush[,] pulling up all Stones great and Small that Can be raised & Carried off the bredth of a Rod[,] and the Limbs of all Trees hanging over the said rodes to be Lopt and Carried off...."[4]

A debate over what exactly constituted one day's labor led to additional clarification of the highway act in 1713. Should a man who brought his team of oxen to work on the road or who provided the use of his wagon be required to work the same number of days as the man who just brought his hands and muscle? The 1713 act defined one day's labor by man and team as equivalent to three days' labor by a man alone. It also elaborated more fully on the responsibilities of the individual laborers. From now on, each farmer was to bring his own "Spades, Axes, Crows, Pick-axes, and other Utensils" for the job of road clear-ance and maintenance.[5]

Roads after the Revolution

After the Revolution, the newly established state and local governments continued to use the same system of roadways and road maintenance set up earlier in the century under colonial rule. Each township elected road commissioners with the power to claim private lands for the public domain and to call upon local residents for annual labor on the roads. Unlike earlier legislation, however, the annual road work quota was no longer fixed by the state. Instead, each township established the number of days required of its inhabitants for road work,

---

(4) "An Act for the Explaining An Act Entituled an Act for the Laying out Regulating Cleer-ing and preserving Publick Common Highways thro'out this Colony," October 30, 1708, *Colonial Laws of New York*, 1:632-633.

(5) "An Act for the further laying out, Regulating and better Clearing Publick High-ways through-out this Colony," October 23, 1713, *Colonial Laws of New York*, 1:795-800.

based on the "estate and ability" of each resident. No one person could be required to work more than 20 days annually. A day's labor was defined as six hours.[6]

The final road legislation of the 18th century established three superintendents of highways for each county. They oversaw, on a county-wide basis, the activities of the road commissioners. The same legislation extended the maximum allowable days of road work required of inhabitants from 20 to 30 days.[7] The rapid growth of traffic on the roads lay at the heart of increased labor assessments for road work and ultimately for increasing tax rates for repairs on bridges and roads throughout the state. A separate apportionment of the annual taxes raised by each township in old Orange County in the 1790s was earmarked for "Bridges and Roads."

In 1795 Hempstead (Ramapo) allocated £26.16.2 for road maintenance, Clarkstown allocated £26.16.2 of its taxes, and Haverstraw allocated £10.5.8. By 1798 the assessments had risen for Hempstead to £33.16.0, for Clarkstown to £33.16.0, for Orangetown to £26.17.0, and for Haverstraw to £16.18.0. The cost of road maintenance as a proportion of the total town budgets had increased dramatically even in this short three-year period. While Hempstead's expenses for roads and bridges remained relatively constant, 14% to 14.5% of the annual budget, other townships experienced far more dramatic increases. Clarkstown's assessment for bridges and road work jumped from 13.7% in 1795 to 31% in 1798. In Haverstraw roadwork accounted for 12.7% of the budget in 1795, but 24.5% in 1798. Orangetown did not have an assessment for roadwork in 1795, but allocated over 32% of its 1798 budget to bridges and roads.[8]

The increased traffic on Rockland's roads mirrored increased activity throughout the state, particularly as more and more people and goods made their way into newly opened central, western, and northern New York lands. The existing system of road construction and main-

---

(6)   "An Act for the better laying out regulating and keeping in repair all common and public highways and private roads in the counties of Ulster, Orange, Dutchess, Washington, Westchester, Albany, and Montgomery," May 4, 1784, Chap. 52, 7th Sess., *Laws of the State of New York*, vol. 1 (Albany, N.Y.: Weed, Parsons, & Co., Printers, 1886), pp. 690-699.

(7)   "An Act to regulate highways," March 21, 1797, Chap. 43, 20th Sess., *Laws of the State of New York*, 4:51-60.

(8)   "Orange County, N.Y. Board of Supervisors Proceedings, 1723-1798," Budke Collection, BC-9, The New York Public Library, pp. 347, 366.

tenance could no longer meet the needs of constantly increasing traffic. Private entrepreneurs throughout the state responded with the creation of turnpike corporations. Turnpikes, unlike the public or common highways of the state, were built and maintained by private individuals licensed by the state. In return for building a new road or taking over the maintenance on an existing roadway, the turnpike company had the right to set up toll stations along the road. Turnpikes would really come into their own as an integral part of the New York highway system in the first quarter of the 19th century.

One of the chief culprits in the ever-increasing cost of road maintenance throughout the state was the lack of standardization in the wagons and carts using the roads. In an era of dirt surfaces prone to frequent washouts, thick mud in the spring thaw and autumn rains, as well as heavy dust clouds in areas with heavy traffic, the fact that vehicles did not have a common axle width meant that road surfaces were constantly being torn up. This placed an even greater burden on the local road crews. The 1797 law that created the position of superintendent of highways also required that in the future all wagons in New York would be constructed with axles of a uniform width. Starting on September 1, 1797, all wagons made in New York State would be built so that "when the wheels are placed upon the axletrees, the outside of the fellows of two wheels on the same axletree shall not be less than five feet asunder."[9] Legislators hoped that such standardization would keep the roads from being cut up by the much narrower widths of many of the wagons already in use throughout the state.

Increased road usage also led legislators to create a new system of mileage markers on all the principal roadways in the state. The superintendents of highways in each county set up "stones or posts" along one side of the major post roads "at the distance of one mile from each other." At the same time the superintendents had guideposts placed at the intersections of all the post roads in the state and at all side roads leading to any town, village, or landing. This new system of signage, with both mileage and directional signs for towns and villages, was necessary because more and more strangers were using the local roads. The original lanes and paths had been created almost entirely

---

(9)   "An Act to regulate highways," March 21, 1797, p. 60.

by and for local custom. By the end of the 18th century, Orange and Rockland counties saw greater numbers of travelers passing through or visiting the area. These strangers did not know the local landmarks and needed guideposts to navigate the area. At the same time, the mileposts enabled passengers on the rapidly expanding system of stage routes throughout the state to keep track of their mileage. This helped keep arguments between stage drivers and passengers to a minimum since fees were based on miles traveled.

Travel by Stage Wagon

Although the most popular stage line along the Hudson ran up the east side of the river between New York City and Albany, Rocklanders in the Ramapo Valley west of New Antrim (Suffern) also had an opportunity to become familiar with the awkward stage wagons of the late 18th century. In the spring of 1797 Rockland residents saw

Engraving, "American Stage Waggon," James Storer after Isaac Weld, from Weld, *Travels Through the States of North America...during 1795, 1796 and 1797,* London, 1798.
Rare Books and Manuscripts Division, The New York Public Library.

their first local stage line when New York State granted Anthony Dobbin and James Tustin of Goshen a three-year monopoly to run a stage wagon between Goshen and New York City. Dobbin and Tustin had to provide one good covered stage wagon drawn by four horses for the proposed stage route. It would run from Goshen through the pass in the Ramapo Mountains to New Antrim, then continue south into New Jersey for the final leg to Paulus Hook and the ferry to New York City. Much of it followed the same path laid in 1703 for the Albany Road. The cost per passenger was not to exceed 4¢ per mile. This included 14 pounds of baggage per person. The stage wagon had to make the trip between New York and Goshen at least once a week, barring impassable roads.[10]

The stage wagons used on this and other early stage lines were just that, wagons with benches and a canvas top suspended from poles attached to the outside of the wagon. A 1795 description of travel aboard a stage wagon is representative of these early vehicles. The wagon was

> a long car with four benches. Three of these in the interior held nine passengers. A tenth passenger was seated by the side of the driver on the front bench. A light roof was supported by eight slender pillars, four on each side. Three large leather curtains suspended to the roof, one at each side and the third behind, were rolled up or lowered at the pleasure of the passengers. There was no place nor space for luggage, each person being expected to stow his things as he could under his seat or legs. The entrance was in front over the driver's bench. Of course the three passengers on the back seat were obliged to crawl across all the other benches to get to their places. There were no backs to the benches to support and relieve us during the rough and fatiguing journey over a newly and ill-made road.[11]

---

(10) "An Act granting to Anthony Dobbin and James Tustin the exclusive right of running stage waggons and other carriages between the town of Goshen and the city of New York," March 30, 1797, Chap. 70, 20th Sess., *Laws of the State of New York*, 4:97-98.

(11) Thomas Twining, as quoted in Alice Morse Earle, *Stage-Coach & Tavern Days* (1900; reprint, New York: Dover Publications, Inc., 1969), p. 262.

The lack of any kind of cushioning or back support made the back bench the best seat. At least here the passenger could lean against the back of the wagon.

Free-floating luggage also inflicted its share of suffering upon the unsuspecting passenger. Hand luggage, mail, and other small items shared the limited floor space "to the great annoyance of the passengers, who are frequently forced to sit with their knees up to their mouths, or with their feet insinuated between two trunks, where they are most lovingly compressed whenever the vehicle makes a lurch into a rut."[12]

The ever-growing use of the road system in Orange and Rockland counties and the rest of New York permitted the movement of people further and further away from the principal waterways that had provided the main routes of transportation during the 17th and much of the 18th century. The Hudson and Mohawk river valleys had traditionally provided access to the interior of New York, and settlements obviously expanded inland from these key transportation links. The defeat of the British during the American Revolution meant that their Native American allies in western, central, and northern New York could be forced off their ancestral lands. Unlike the areas settled earlier in the 17th and 18th centuries, these newly opened lands had few navigable waterways to facilitate access. A land-based transportation network became a necessity. For many years the roads along the Hudson had been an adjunct to the river, providing local communication between farms and hamlets and giving access to the river landings. They had received their greatest use during the winter months when the rivers froze and snowy conditions allowed for the use of sleighs for people and sleds for hauling.

Land Travel Versus Water Travel

By the 1780s and 1790s, the wholesale movement of people over land made the roadways a primary transportation system rather than the support system they had played earlier. The rapid expansion of stage

(12) John M. Duncan, as quoted in Ulysses Prentiss Hedrick, *A History of Agriculture in the State of New York* (Albany, N.Y.: New York State Agricultural Society, 1933), p. 172. See illustration by James Storer after Isaac Weld (1774-1856), "American Stage Waggon," engraved plate in Weld's *Travels Through the States of North America...during 1795, 1796, and 1797*, London, 1798.

lines during this same period underscored the increasing importance of the road system over the rivers. Transportation on the rivers remained at the mercy of the winds and tides. A trip up the Hudson on a Hudson River sloop from New York City to Albany could take anywhere from two to six days, depending on weather conditions. Once the stage lines were established, they made the trip in two days, twice a week, on the east side of the river. They also made the trip year round, unlike river traffic that closed down in December when the river froze around Albany and remained closed for three to four months, depending on the severity of the winter. The U.S. mail quickly turned to the stage lines as the licensed postal carriers because they promised more reliable, year-round service.

The substitution of sled runners for wheels allowed New York's stage wagons to travel the snow- and ice-covered roadways during the cold winter months. Coaches had minimal suspension systems. It was fairly easy to remove the wheels and replace them with runners. Francisco de Miranda, a Latin American soldier who visited the Hudson Valley in the winter of 1783-1784, thought of this transformation as though fitting the stage wagon "with skates rather than wheels, forming a great sledge, covered with a painted canvas for protection." Once outfitted with runners, the transformed wagons carried "ten passengers, two coachmen, and twelve hundredweights of baggage — all went on the one sledge, drawn by four horses and traveling nine to ten miles per hour."[13]

It was during these winter months, when the ground was frozen and snow blanketed the roads and fields, that land transportation really came into its own. Pleasure sleighs and work sleds dotted the roadways, with the tinkling of harness bells keeping everyone alert for fast-approaching horse and sleigh. The really heavy hauling of freight, lumber, stones, etc., could best be accomplished by sled. The frozen ground and slick, snow-covered roadways facilitated the movement of heavy loads that would bog down in the spring mud and simply would not move over the heavily rutted roads of summer and fall.

---

(13)   Francisco de Miranda, *The New Democracy in America: Travels of Francisco de Miranda in the United States, 1783-1784*, trans. Judson P. Wood, ed. John S. Ezell (Norman, Okla.: University of Oklahoma Press, 1963), p .69.

The Roads of Rockland County in the 1790s

> Monday, the 26th [April 1742]....The mountains here
> are the most brushy and rockey [*sic*] I ever saw, full of
> Laurels and underwood....When we finished this lott
> sent to Mr. Smiths for some of our provisions which we
> left there, for we could bring no more with us into the
> mountains than a man carried on his back, it being
> impossible for a horse to follow us over the vast hills.
>
> Friday the 30th....the mountain here is miserable trav-
> elling being so full of Laurel and brush....[14]

The few roads that crossed Rockland County at the end of the
18th century were little more than rutted lanes, wide enough for a cart
or wagon if necessary but much more frequently traversed by horse or
by foot. Most roads connected farms and hamlets, meandering in
response to shifts in the landscape or going around cleared fields.
Despite the growth of overland traffic in the 1790s as more and more
settlers moved into central New York, the majority of Rockland
County's traffic was local. Narrow lanes connected farmsteads to the
public highways that in themselves were little more than winding tracts
through the rocky hills and woodlands that covered the county.

There were several principal north-south paths winding their
way along the small river valleys and between the mountains. People
and goods traveling between the northern and southern parts of Rockland generally had four possible land routes. The easternmost road,
another King's Road, ran from Tappan north, going to the west of
Rockland Lake (called Quaspeck Pond), down through the Long Clove
in Hook Mountain to enter the hamlet of Haverstraw, then to King's
Ferry (Stony Point) and beyond to Albany (#1 on map, page 25). The
westernmost inland route, also called the Military Highway because of
its importance during the American Revolution, connected New Antrim
with King's Ferry. It went through the inland valley between the

---

(14)   Charles Clinton, field notes on surveys of the Cheesecocks Patent, as quoted in Cole,
       History of Rockland County, pp. 159, 161.

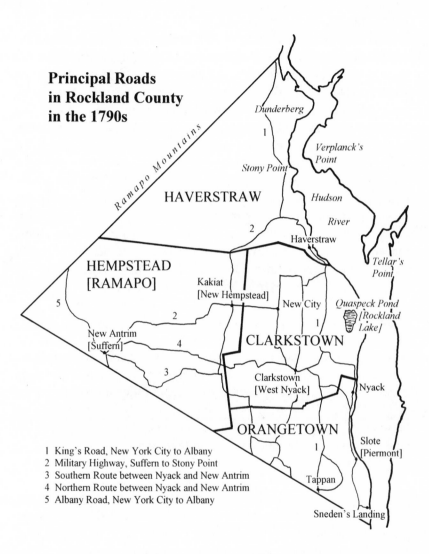

**Principal Roads
in Rockland County
in the 1790s**

Ramapo Mountains

Dunderberg

1

*Verplanck's
Point*

Stony Point

HAVERSTRAW

Hudson

2

River

Haverstraw

*Tellar's
Point*

**HEMPSTEAD
[RAMAPO]**

Kakiat
[New Hempstead]

New City

*Quaspeck Pond
[Rockland
Lake]*

5

2

1

New Antrim
[Suffern]

4

CLARKSTOWN

3

Clarkstown
[West Nyack]

Nyack

ORANGETOWN

1

Slote
[Piermont]

1 King's Road, New York City to Albany
2 Military Highway, Suffern to Stony Point
3 Southern Route between Nyack and New Antrim
4 Northern Route between Nyack and New Antrim
5 Albany Road, New York City to Albany

Tappan

Sneden's Landing

Verdrietig Hook on the east and the Ramapo Mountains on the west. Minisceongo Creek meandered between the two mountains near the Clarkstown/Hempstead border. The road generally followed the creek valley from Haverstraw to Kakiat in Hempstead Township. The road then twisted and turned in a generally southwesterly direction until it came to John Suffern's store and tavern at New Antrim. From here the traveler could either turn to the north for Goshen or Newburgh, or go south into New Jersey (#2). Two other routes ran between these paths, one connected Clarkstown with Haverstraw, via the Long Clove. The second route came from further south in the county, midway between Nyack and New Antrim. The road ran north to New City, then down to the Long Clove and on to Haverstraw.

East-west routes were even more limited. The Ramapo Mountains on the west almost completely shut down travel into the interior, focusing transportation along the north-south river axis. The principal exceptions were a collection of meandering farm lanes and Indian trails that could be linked to form a northern and southern route from Nyack on the Hudson to New Antrim and the Ramapo Pass beyond. A narrow, steep track led westward from Nyack, connecting it to the King's Road coming out of Tappan. However, the Greenbush, a large swampy area to the west of the King's Road stopped further direct westward travel at this point. Instead, the traveler could turn south, go around the swamp and then meander westward to New Antrim along old farm lanes and Indian trails (#3). Or he could circumvent the swamp by turning north, then angle west to New Antrim, again following various lanes and trails (#4). Because of the swamp, the roughly 12½-mile distance between Nyack and New Antrim was extended to 18 miles along the southern route and 16 miles on the northern route.[15]

In the second quarter of the 19th century, the Nyack Turnpike successfully traversed the swamp, cutting four to six miles off the 18th-century routes. This would prove particularly important to the iron industries of the Ramapo Mountains. The Nyack Turnpike would significantly reduce the transportation costs for these industries, enabling them to cart their product due east to the Hudson.

One other principal east-west route existed. This road connected

(15) Survey for the Nyack Turnpike taken November 12-13, 1817 by Tunis Smith, Collections of The Historical Society of Rockland County, A88.10.2.

the New Antrim-Haverstraw route with the site of the county seat at New City. The New City Road ran from Kakiat in Hempstead straight eastward to the New City courthouse. Travelers could then work their way north and east down to the Long Clove and Haverstraw, or they could go south and then east to Nyack and Tappan.

The road northward from New Antrim through the Ramapo Pass, or Clove, toward Goshen was the old Albany Road, the last of the principal roads in 18th-century Rockland County (#5). The Orange Turnpike Company, the first turnpike company incorporated by the state, acquired the rights to maintain a portion of this important roadway in 1800. In exchange, the company set up toll booths along the length of the turnpike. The turnpike led from New Antrim into the interior of New York, following the old road as far as Southfields, where it departed toward Monroe. This roadway became increasingly important in the 19th century as more and more settlers moved inland through the mountains.

Industrial development in the Ramapo Mountains, begun at the Ringwood ironworks in New Jersey and the Sterling ironworks in Orange County in the 18th century, made this a key area for the prosperity of Rockland County. The mountains may have been unattractive to farmers, in many cases almost impassable, but the iron industry brought both wealth and jobs to this desolate area. When Josiah G. Pierson and his brother Jeremiah bought land in the Ramapo Valley in 1795, they began a new era for western Rockland. The Piersons owned a cut nail manufactory in New York City and bought land in the Ramapo Valley to build a new factory. The abundance of wood for charcoal used in the smelting of iron and of water for power made the Ramapo site an ideal location. By 1798 the J. G. Pierson & Brothers had a rolling mill, slitting mill, and nail factory.[16] Although the Piersons imported most of their iron from Russia, they also used small quantities from the Sterling and Ringwood works just a few miles away. Thus the Orange Turnpike, and the earlier Albany to New York City road through the Ramapo Pass were vital to the transport of goods and people through to New York's interior and the iron-rich areas of New York and New Jersey.

---

(16) Cole, *History of Rockland County*, pp. 273-274.

Ferries across the Hudson

Although various roadways successfully linked different areas of Rockland County, the most important links were those which enabled people and products to reach the Hudson River and the New York City market. Landings at Tappan Slote on the Spar Kill and at Haverstraw as well as one mid-county at Slawter's (Slaughter's) Landing near Rockland Lake had docks for small vessels such as periaugers[17] and some Hudson River sloops. In addition, there were two ferry crossings on the Hudson that facilitated commerce and travel between Rocklanders and their neighbors in Westchester County. Dobbs' Ferry ran between Dobbs Ferry in Westchester and Palisades, or Sneden's Landing, in southernmost Rockland. In the north, King's Ferry ran between Stony Point and Verplanck's Point, south of Peekskill. This ferry had been particularly important during the Revolutionary War and formed one terminus of the Military Highway mentioned above.

In 1800 the desire for increased communication between Westchester and Rockland counties resulted in the establishment of another ferry across the Hudson. In March 1800 the state legislature passed "An Act establishing and regulating a ferry across the Hudson river between the counties of Westchester and Rockland."[18] Joseph Travis in Peekskill and Joshua Colwill in the Town of Haverstraw received a 21-year monopoly to "set up, keep and maintain" a ferry across the Hudson. The legislation did not identify the route the ferry would take, but one is known to have run between the base of the Dunderberg at Caldwell's Landing (Jones Point) and Peekskill.

Travis and Colwill each had to provide a convenient dock or landing place for a ferry as well as a ferry boat capable of conveying six horses. The ferriage rates, established by law, were: 50¢ for horse and rider; 75¢ for one-horse sulky or chair with passenger; $1.25 for wagon and load, with passengers, drawn by two horses; $1.25 for four-wheel carriages with two horses (chariots) and passengers; and 32¢ for a foot passenger. This ferry served local traffic between

---

(17)   Periauger: a small sailing vessel used for short trips along the Hudson. Frequently carried cargo, but smaller than a sloop.

(18)   Chap. 28, 23rd Sess., *Laws of the State of New York*, 4:472-473.

Westchester and Rockland rather than the stage lines on the post roads. As a result there was no established ferry rate for coaches with four horses, the typical stage wagon or coach. The stage lines crossed the Hudson between New York City and Paulus Hook in New Jersey and then headed north along the Orange Turnpike toward Goshen and Albany.

Although these ferries were intended to run year-round, winter river crossings meant particularly hazardous conditions. The Hudson between Westchester and Rockland froze during the winter months, but it seldom froze solid. The ferries could not run at these times, so travelers crossed on foot or in wagons, with sometimes deadly results. Travelers were advised to get off any carriage or wagon that was about to cross a stream and let the horses and carriage lead the way. Invariably, some people decided to remain in the carriage and if the ice broke, they drowned. Reports of several such drownings, including one off Tarrytown in Westchester and one off Tappan in Rockland, appeared in 18th-century news accounts.

> By the Albany Post, we hear of several Accidents on Persons crossing the North River [Hudson] on the Ice: At Poughkeepsie two horses in [and] a sleigh, were drown'd, about 10 Days ago, and another near Philipse's Upper Mills [Sleepy Hollow]; and on Tuesday last, a Sleigh with three or four People in it, was observed to go on the River in order to cross it, a little above Tappan; and on comming [sic] near the Middle on a drive, fell in and were no more seen.[19]

Such occurrences were common between Rockland and Westchester when the ferries could not run. Passengers or livestock occasionally might fall overboard during spring, summer, and fall crossings, but at least then the danger was limited to drowning rather than freezing and drowning.

---

(19) *The New-York Gazette and Weekly Post-Boy*, January 27, 1752.

River Transportation, a Slow but Steady Alternative

> The beauties of the North River consist in the bold-
> ness of its banks, the extensive sheet sometimes seen
> before one, & the numerous small vessels which are
> continuously to be seen plying backwards & forwards.
> Upwards of 2000 sail, [much] of which from 10 to 50 tons,
> are exclusively employed on this river in removing the
> produce from the interior to the City & supply the inland
> population with necessaries.[20]

Although J.B. Dunlop made this comment in 1811, it was accu-
rate for the end of the 18th century and would remain true for most of
the 19th century. The roads of Rockland linked the farms and hamlets
with one another and offered an avenue through the mountains and into
the interior of Orange County. The Hudson, or North River, remained
the principal thoroughfare for the transport of goods between New York
and Albany. With the exception of the winter months, when river traffic
was shut down by ice, the Hudson offered the only economically viable
means of transporting heavy freight to and from New York. Sending
heavy cargoes of grain, iron ore, or manufactured goods by wagon
overland quickly transformed relatively smooth road surfaces into
rutted quagmires and increased road maintenance costs for local households. If these same goods could be carted to a dock along the Hudson
and loaded aboard a sloop, they would be moved more rapidly, with
less breakage, and more cheaply. Freight charges on Hudson River
sloops in 1800 ranged from $2.50 to $3.00 a ton. [21] Land rates could
not begin to compete

Accommodations for River Travelers

If it was cheap to send freight up and down the Hudson, passenger fares between Albany and New York were also quite reasonable.
In 1795 the basic fare between Albany and New York City was 10

---

(20) J.B. Dunlop, "'From the Windows of the Mail Coach' A Scotsman Looks at New York
      State in 1811," ed. David H. Wallace, *The New-York Historical Society Quarterly*, XL
      (July 1956), pp. 273-274.
(21) John S. Curtiss, "The Sloops of the Hudson, 1800-1850," *New York History*, XIV (Jan.
      1933), p. 69.

shillings, or $1.25. By 1800 it had risen to $2. If a traveler wanted a bed for the night with food and beverage provided for the voyage, that would cost an additional $4.50.[22] If a passenger preferred to take the stage line, he or she would pay fourpence a mile.[23] On the Albany Post Road on the east side of the Hudson, this would run at least $3.75 for 120 miles, probably a conservative estimate.

The trade-offs between the stage and the sloop were clear. The stage line offered reliable, scheduled service between Albany and New York that ran year-round. It was favored by businessmen who needed to reach their destination at a specific time and by local travelers going relatively short distances between towns. The sloops, on the other hand, offered considerably more comfort but a schedule that had to be very flexible.

The comfort came from a large, roomy cabin that could accommodate the paying customer with a dinner table, comfortable chairs, and even beds for the overnight traveler. Isaac Weld sailed between New York and Albany aboard one of these Hudson River sloops in the summer of 1796. He found the accommodations more than satisfactory, particularly as he was intent on enjoying the scenery:

> Our sloop was not more than seventy tons burthen by register; but the accommodations she afforded were most excellent, and far superior to what might be expected on board so small a vessel; the cabin was equally large with that in a common merchant vessel of three hundred tons, built for crossing the ocean. This was owing to the great breadth of her beam, which was no less than twenty-two feet and a half, although her length was only fifty-five feet. All the sloops engaged in this trade are built nearly on the same construction; short, broad, and very shallow, few of them draw more than

(22) Curtiss, p. 65.
(23) Mileage figure is based on the fare from Claverack to Albany on October 24, 1785 in Alexander Coventry, "Memoirs of an Emigrant: The Journal of Alexander Coventry, M.D. in Scotland, the United States, and Canada during the Period 1783-1831," prepared by the Albany Institute of History and Art and the New York State Library, 2 vols., 1978, pp. 82-83.

five or six feet water, so that they are only calculated for sailing upon smooth water.[24]

Weld's voyage went swiftly. He departed New York at 2 p.m. on July 2 and arrived in Albany at 4 a.m. on July 4. In this he was quite fortunate. The sloop was not only at the mercy of the fickle winds that constantly shifted as the Hudson cut its way from the interior of New York to the sea but also of the tides. The Hudson is tidal all the way to Albany, and the sloops generally had to lie at anchor when the tide ran against them, particularly if the winds failed. If everything went right, the voyage between New York and Albany should have taken 26 hours. However, it very seldom went right.

Mme. de la Tour du Pin, a French émigré who settled in New York State, had sailed from Albany to New York in 1795. She boarded her vessel at night, intent on leaving on high tide that occurred in the early morning hours. Despite a propitious start, her trip took over 48 hours. Like Weld, she appreciated the amenities aboard her sloop, the "good cabins and a pretty saloon."[25] She also wasn't in a hurry. Peter Kalm's 1748 voyage from New York to Albany took nearly 72 hours.[26] If time was of the essence, the river was not the way to travel.

Weld, Kalm, and Mme. de la Tour du Pin traveled the equivalent of first class. They would have paid that extra $4.50 for bed and board during the trip. They probably also brought along any special food or beverages that they might want. Most travelers simply paid for their passage and provided their own food and drink. At night they bedded down on the deck as best they could. During those periods when the sloop was becalmed or when it was at anchor waiting for the tide to turn, passengers sometimes added to any food and drink that they had brought aboard by rowing over to a local farm. A brief visit to a farm along the river could provide fresh milk or butter, possibly fruit, depending on the season.

---

(24) Isaac Weld, Jr., *Travels through the States of North America and the Provinces of Upper & Lower Canada during the Years 1795, 1796, 1797,* 4th ed. (1807), 2 vols. (New York: Augustus M. Kelley, 1970), 1:269.

(25) *Memoirs of Madame de la Tour du Pin,* ed. and trans. Felice Harcourt, introd. Peter Gay, 1st Amer. ed. (New York: McCall Publishing Co., 1971), pp. 270, 272.

(26) *Travels into North America,* pp. 316-322.

A Rocklander Travels by Land and by Water

David Pye (1724-1804) of Clarkstown kept a diary in 1784-1785 in which he recorded many of his activities for the year. An English immigrant who came to New York in 1757, Pye had settled in the Clarkstown area in the 1760s. By the mid-1780s he was a man of considerable importance in his neighborhood and made several trips each year to New York City. Depending on conditions, he traveled either by land or by water.

In the fall of 1784 he and Theodore Snedeker boarded Coleman's boat and arrived in New York City on the afternoon of November 7. Pye went to New York to hear Doctor Clark preach. Once in New York, he stayed a little over a week on various errands, then sailed back to Rockland. He left the evening of the 16th aboard Captain Smith's vessel, possibly a sloop, and landed at Nyack on the morning of the 17th. He was back home before noon.

A month later Pye again planned a trip to New York City. On December 21 he was "making ready to go to N. York and at noon went to Nyack to Mr. Corneilsons" and then "to Slote, lodged at Wandle's." He intended to leave the next morning from Slote, but it was stormy and the "petrager" did not make the trip.

Pye's trip to the city was postponed until February 3, when Abraham Blauvelt and John Wallace stopped by on their way to New York. Pye decided to accompany them, but this time they went by land. The river was frozen. They sledded down the Old King's Road to Hoboken where they spent the night. The next morning they took a ferry across the Hudson to New York, arriving about 10 a.m. Pye remained in the city for five days, then returned, this time with Abraham Blauvelt and John Van Orden. They crossed the Hudson in the afternoon and spent the night at Closter, New Jersey. Pye sledded home the next day, stopping at several farms along the way. He arrived home in the evening of the 10th.

River traffic still was not moving three weeks later when Pye returned to New York once again, this time traveling with Abraham Mabie of Orangetown. They left in the morning and arrived in the afternoon of March 8. Pye chose to return home on the Sabbath, something that was still generally frowned upon. He crossed the Hudson at Paulus Hook and traveled up through New Jersey on the Old

King's Road, arriving home "before Evening."

David Pye made two more trips to the city during the spring of 1785, each about a month apart. It is not clear how he traveled for the April 7-11 trip, but the May 6-8 trip was again made by boat. As on his February trip, he returned on the Sabbath, this time using the periauger that landed at Slote.[27]

David Pye does not say why he made these five trips to New York between November 1784 and May 1785, but he evidently preferred to travel by water when possible. If the winds and tide cooperated, he could make the trip in relative comfort in a few hours. If he came over land he would have used the ferry at Paulus Hook, a two-and-a-half-mile ferry crossing that could take an hour by itself. Henry Wansey, an English traveler, found the ferry crossing trying, even in the summer months:

> I crossed Hudson's River at Paulus-hook, to take the stage on the other side for Philadelphia. Though only two miles and a half across, we were an hour and a half passing, owing to the rapidity of the current, from the violent storm the day before. I paid five dollars, and went in the stage called the Industry.[28]

David Pye would not have faced the swift current that accompanied spring storms, but his would have been a winter crossing with ice floating in the river, the cold February and March winds blowing. He then sledded between Paulus Hook and his home in Clarkstown. Traveling by land did have one advantage, however. It gave Pye the opportunity to stop in and visit with acquaintances in New Jersey and Orangetown as he traveled along the Old King's Road.

Pye was not a typical Rockland farmer. He was a prominent member of the community. He became the first county clerk of Rockland (1798 until his death in 1804), having already represented the Rockland area in the state assembly and senate. He farmed his lands

---

(27) *Pye Genealogy and Diary of David Pye*, comp. Walter Leonard Pye, additions by George Henry Budke, 1921, Budke Collection, BC-88a, The New York Public Library, Manuscripts & Archives Division (Library Association of Rockland County, 1975), *passim*. [Hereafter referred to as *David Pye Diary*.]

(28) *Henry Wansey and His American Journal, 1794*, ed. David John Jeremy (Philadelphia: American Philosophical Society, 1970), June 4, 1794, p. 90.

DAVID PYE, ESQ.
1724 -- 1804

David Pye (1724-1804). Budke Collection, BC-88a, Rare Books and
Manuscripts Division, The New York Public Library.

in Clarkstown, but he was not just a farmer. Mechanically adept, he owned and operated a fulling mill and fixed his neighbors' watches and clocks. He had won his neighbors' confidence with his skill as a surveyor and was frequently called upon to draw up legal documents, such as wills and deeds. He undoubtedly traveled around the county and outside the county much more frequently than those Rocklanders who lived by farming alone.

But his choices of route and method were just as limited. He could travel by foot, by horse, by sled or wagon, or by boat. He used any and all these methods as appropriate. When traveling north and south in the county, he could select from several different routes. All these routes, however, had to funnel either through the Long Clove near the river just south of Haverstraw, or they had to go up the valley between the Ramapo Mountains on the west and Verdreitig Hook on the east. If he wanted to travel inland, toward Goshen, he had to go to New Antrim and then travel the old Albany Road through the Ramapo Pass and into Orange County proper. The mountains and the river circumscribed the transportation options available to David Pye and all the other residents of Rockland.

Chapter 3

ॐ

Life in
an Agricultural
Community

Eighteenth of Feby 1793

Then I was Noculated for the small Pocks By Doctor
Abm Cornelison in the house of Garret I Blauvelt on a
Monday about 2 o Clock in the afternoon with my Brother
and seven others, there were two Blacks amoung us[.] the
same Evening we had to take one Pill Each and Black two
a Piece which workit us Downwardly in the next morning.
on thuesday some of them Got Noculated again[.] in the
Evening we had to take some white stuff mixt with water
and the next morning again which made us all feel sick
and some spewed[.] we Continued taking this stuff till
friday eveng and on saturday we went out a Guning And
shot two Squirrels And two Quails[.] on sunday some of
us Look't very Drowsy[.] On Monday 25th we began to
be very Cold[.] in the afternoon I and Corns went to Abrm
T. to see how they Came on there for they were noculated
two Days after us[.] we went on horse-Back but Rode
very sober[.] At night I began to be very Sick and they all
Crowded to the fire but Did not want to to [sic] fetch in
wood[.] I Remaind Sick till the 28th then my Pocks Began
to Come out[.] I had the Rash very full and so had my
Brother before the Pocks came out[.] they kept Comeing

37

A Carpenter.   W.R. sc.

Reproduced from the Collections of the Library of Congress.

out for four or five Days[.]   on Saturday the second of
March we went out again and shot 5 Pigeons[.] on Sunday
our throats began to be very sore[.]   I had it so bad that if
I Drank water it Run out my nose[.]   this Staid so till the
Pocks began to Dry[.]   I had about seventy on my face
and on my Body Accordingly[.]   my Brother and Gitty sot
[got?] very full[.]   I suppose they had each five or six
Hundred on their faces But my Brothers Dried very fast[.]
he beat Gitty five or six Days.   On friday the 8th some of
them Got Purged off and on sunday I was Purged off and
on thues Day following Peter Purg'd of[f] and on thursdy
the 16th I went home and staid home[.]   our Diet was no
salt or fresh meat or Pork no sweet milk or Butter until we
were Purg'd of[f.]   I staid in the Back Room away from
my mother and Peter Came home on Monday following.
we staid there Each about a fortenet & then Pased free
amoung other People.[1]

When Tunis Smith wasn't spending six weeks protecting
himself from the deadly perils of smallpox, his life revolved
around the seasons, not the clock, and the weather, not an
inflexible schedule. Tunis Smith, of Tappan, was 21 when he and his
younger brother Peter entered Garret I. Blauvelt's house to undergo the
debilitating but effective inoculation process. They spent six weeks
recovering from a self-induced bout with cow pox, a less virulent cousin
of the smallpox virus, that gave them immunity to smallpox itself. Once
recovered, they could carry on with their lives as the sons of a Tappan
farmer, learning a variety of skills and talents to supplement the basic
economic activity of Rockland, i.e., farming.

(1)   Tunis Smith, "Remembrance," Salisbury Papers, *Historical Miscellanies*, collected and
comp. George H. Budke, I, 1923, Budke Collection, BC-70, The New York Public
Library, Manuscripts & Archives Division (Library Association of Rockland County,
1975), pp. 49-50.

Tunis had received about seven years of schooling from the local schoolmaster. Then at the age of 13 he "Learnt the weavers trade and wove & work't on the Farm untill I was about sixteen years old."[2] Between the fall of 1788 and 1791 he served as schoolmaster in Greenbush (Blauvelt), then briefly returned to weaving. In the spring of 1792 he added surveying to his marketable skills, then took over as schoolmaster for the Township of Clarkstown for one quarter. By July 1792 he had had enough of teaching and decided to return to weaving and surveying as a livelihood. All this just as he reached the age of 20.

This learning of different skills, particularly weaving and surveying, made Tunis a more valuable member of his farming community. They were, however, skills that would be used when he had free time from the primary economic focus of Rockland, the farm.

Once free of the illness and quarantine of inoculation, Tunis, with his father, bought his first stallion for £24 and kept an accounting of the mares serviced for his neighbors at 16 shillings a mare. His "Remembrance" goes on to give the Fourth of July 1793 as the beginning of the rye harvest that lasted four days. The wheat harvest was finished and buckwheat put in the following week. By mid-August Tunis, his father, and his brother were mowing the salt meadow and stacking the salt hay. At the end of the month they sowed rye once again. September saw Tunis mowing the buckwheat, which was threshed in October. Tending the fields and the crops to ensure enough food and forage for the family and their livestock to get through the winter was the most important job for a rural New York resident. The skills of weaving and surveying would be applied during slack periods, when the crops did not need tending.

The Smith family enterprises expanded into milling in the winter and spring of 1795 while the fields lay dormant under winter ice and snow. Tunis and his father began cutting timber for the mill in January, timber that could be sledded easily over the frozen fields to the mill stream. The carpenter arrived in mid-April, raising the mill-house frame in 11 days. Tunis and his father ran the mill jointly for the next seven years. Then his father retired to live with Peter, splitting his lands into two farms, with Peter getting the "old farm" while Tunis got the farm he currently worked as well as the saw mill.

---

(2)   "Remembrance," p. 49.

This interweaving of farming with other activities typified life in Rockland throughout the 18th and well into the 19th centuries. In fact, it is the basic nature of life in any farming community, anywhere in the world. The farming activities must be taken care of first, then other skills, other interests, other concerns can be indulged. The need to accomplish the sowing, the harvesting, the threshing is foremost. So is the need to breed livestock to ensure future generations of food stock and work stock. The sheep have to be sheared each spring, or the wool is ruined. Killing time came late each fall, or the family might lack food for the winter. If these tasks were not completed properly, the family would suffer, there would not be enough fodder for the livestock to be wintered over, and starvation would spread into the barn as well as the farmhouse.

Tunis Smith and David Pye, the only late 18th-century Rockland residents to leave us an account of their day-to-day lives, mixed farming activities with other endeavors that served the interests and needs of their agricultural world. Their accounts can be meshed with other 18th-century references to farming in New York and neighboring New England to provide a glimpse of the seasonal pacing of life in the 1790s. The Rev. Silas Constant, a Presbyterian minister in Yorktown, across the Hudson in Westchester County, kept a journal of his daily activities from 1784 to 1825 that freely intersperses ministerial duties with running a farm.[3] William Strickland, a British agriculturist, toured New York and neighboring areas in 1794-1795 and published his observations on agricultural practices in the new United States, providing an outsider's impressions of farming in the Hudson River Valley at the end of the 18th century.[4] During these same years the first American guide to farming in the United States was published. Samuel Deane's *Georgical Dictionary* provided detailed instructions on all aspects of farming in the Northeast.[5]

(3)   Emily Warren Roebling, *The Journal of the Rev. Silas Constant, Pastor of the Presbyterian Church at Yorktown, New York, with some of the Records of the Church and a List of his Marriages, 1784-1825, together with Notes on the Nelson, Van Cortlandt, Warren, and some other Families mentioned in the Journal*, ed. Josiah Granville Leach, L.L.B. (Philadelphia: J.B. Lippincott Co., 1903).

(4)   William Strickland, *Journal of a Tour in the United States of America, 1794-1795*, ed. Rev. J.E. Strickland (New York: The New-York Historical Society, 1971).

(5)   Samuel Deane, D.D., *The New England Farmer; or Georgical Dictionary, containing a Compendious Account of the Ways and Methods in that the Important Art of Husbandry, in all its Various Branches, Is, or May Be, Practised, to the Greatest Advantage, in this Country*, 2nd ed. (Worcester, Mass.: at the press of Isaiah Thomas, 1797).

Life in a Farming Community in the 1790s: The Seasons

The rocky land on the west shore, extends to Tappan Bay where the river expands to about 3½ miles. The land is little cultivated except some spots around the houses, some of which are neat and have good appearance, but most of them only small huts, but the orchards and other trees, which cast a shade about the houses, render the meanest of them very agreeable to the eye. Some of the neatest of them have pavilions, covered with vines, extending around the houses.[6]

The plough, seen here in a late 18th-century American engraving, was the Rockland farmer's most important tool. Detail, engraving, "Venerate the Plough," American farm scene, late 18th century, *Columbian Magazine*.
    Rare Books and Manuscripts Division, The New York Public Library.

---

(6)   Alexander Coventry, "Memoirs of an Emigrant," September 14, 1785, p. 70.

Spring:
April, May, and June

It is the most busy and hurrying season, for farmers in this country, of any in the year; partly owing to the long continuance of frost, which commonly prevents all kinds of tillage till near the beginning of April; and in the northern parts, till the end of the month. But sometimes it is partly owing also to what we might order otherwise, to sowing a larger proportion than is necessary of our grain in the spring, and neglecting in the autumn to cart out so much of our manure as we might, that we complain of being so much hurried with work in the spring.

But besides tillage and seeding, which are enough to employ the whole time, there are other matters to be attended to at this season. The fences are always to be examined, and repaired: For though they were in good order in the fall preceding, high winds, violent storms, and deep snows, may overset, break or settle them, not to mention the gradual decay and rotting of wooden fences. Or the violence of frost may heave and disorder them. Compost dunghills it will often be needful to make at this season, especially if the materials were not all obtainable in the preceding autumn.[7]

Spring was the time for final preparations for the growing season. Once the frost had left the ground, it needed to be ploughed in preparation for the sowing of the spring crops: barley, peas, oats, flax, summer wheat, then potatoes and corn. Once the fields had been ploughed, with wooden ploughs drawn by horses or oxen through long, narrow fields, the farmer sowed the seed broadcast. Carrying a sack full of seed, he walked down the center of each narrow field. As he walked, he took a handful of grain and cast it out to each side, spreading the seed unevenly over the field. He then covered the seed by dragging a harrow through the field. The harrow might be something as simple

(7)   Deane, *Georgical Dictionary*, p. 314.

as brush dragged behind a horse. Or it might be more elaborate, a triangular wooden A-frame with iron teeth that both pulverized the soil and spread a thin layer of dirt over the freshly sown seed. Each field had to be ploughed, sown, and harrowed to ensure the next year's food supply.[8]

Ploughing the fields was the number one consideration, but other activities had to be carried out at the same time. Fences had to be mended to protect the soon-to-be planted fields from foraging livestock. Fences were designed to keep animals out of planted areas; otherwise they ran free throughout the county. Rockland farmers registered their brands or ear markings with the town officials and then allowed their livestock to roam.

Those livestock, particularly the cattle and sheep, were just finishing up calving and lambing. Farmers wanted their new generation of livestock born in the late winter or early spring so that as soon as they were weaned, they could graze on the new spring grasses. If they were born too soon, they faced the possibility of freezing or starving. If born too late, they might not be sufficiently well grown to survive the next winter. Tunis Smith bought his stallion in April 1793, just in time for the peak breeding period for mares. His neighbors proved eager to use the services of the young stallion. Aurt and John Ramson, Adolphus Smith, James, John and Teunis Blauvelt, John, Isaac, Jacobus and James Perry as well as Teunis T. Tallman and others all paid a stud fee for his stallion's services.[9] These farmers bred their mares in April-June, looking forward to the birth of a new foal in March-June of the following year.

The newly ploughed fields would provide food for the current and next generation of livestock, as well as bread for the table, but the kitchen garden with its unique blending of herbs, flowers, and vegetables also had to be prepared. Although the field crops provided the staples, variety in the 18th-century diet rested on the produce of the garden. As Samuel Deane maintained, "A kitchen garden is almost as necessary to a country seat, as a kitchen to a house: For without one there is no way of being supplied with a great part of necessary food."[10]

(8)   See Jacquetta M. Haley, "Farming in 18th-Century Westchester," *The Westchester Historian*, LXVII (Spring 1991, Summer 1991, Fall 1991), pp. 27-36, 55-65, 83-92; LXVIII (Winter 1992), pp. 12-20, for a detailed account taken from diaries and journals of 18th-century farming in the lower Hudson River Valley. The sources used are from across the river, but the activities are identical to those taking place in Rockland during the same era.
(9)   "Remembrance," pp. 50-51.
(10) *Georgical Dictionary*, pp. 187-188.

Fresh fruits, vegetables, and greens from the kitchen garden gave the farm family badly needed vitamins and minerals, especially after a long winter's diet of bread, dried fruits and vegetables, and salted, smoked, or pickled meats. While the farmer and his sons carried out the heavy work in the kitchen garden, preparing the soil each spring for the new planting, the farmer's wife and daughters generally cared for the kitchen garden.

These three farming activities, ploughing and sowing the fields, overseeing the health of the newest crop of lambs, calves, and foals, and preparing the kitchen garden, took up most of the spring. But other ancillary activities also required attention. David Pye's diary serves as a window onto some of these other activities.[11] Pye had acquired enough wealth and prosperity to employ others to undertake the basic farming tasks. Although he joined his sons and men in the fields when necessary, he was just as likely to be traveling around the county surveying his neighbors' fields or working in his fulling mill.[12]

Role of a Surveyor in a Farming Community

Surveyors played a vital role in farming communities, especially in areas with newly opened lands that had never been settled. Because the source of wealth in any agricultural community is the land, ownership of that land, with clearly defined boundaries, had to be clearly established and maintained. This was the role of the surveyor, who frequently also helped draw up the deeds that transferred the lands he surveyed. David Pye played this role exceedingly well in old Orange County in the 1760s-1780s. He played it so successfully that he had four African slaves by 1790 and had five slaves plus one free black in his household in 1800.[13] His position as a justice of the peace in Orange

---

(11)   *David Pye Diary, passim.*
(12)   A brief biographical sketch of David Pye, Sr., appears in Cole, *History of Rockland County*, p.129.
(13)   *Heads of Families at the First Census of the United States Taken in the Year 1790: New York* (orig. 1908; Baltimore, Md.: Genealogical Publishing Co., Inc., 1992). "Federal Census, 1800: Rockland County, New York," *The New York Genealogical & Biographical Record*, LXI (Oct. 1930), pp. 350-355.

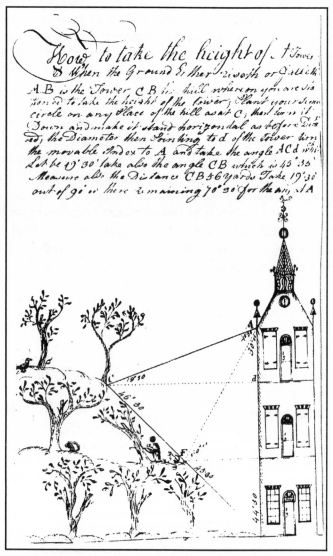

How to take the height of a Tower
& When the Ground Either riseth or falleth
A.B is the Tower CB the hill whereon you are sta
tioned to take the height of the tower; Plant your Semi
circle on any place of the hill as at C, then turn it
Down and make it stand horizondal as before Dire
ted, the Diameter then pointing to d of the Tower turn
the movable Index to A and take the angle ACd which
Let be 19° 30' take also the angle CB which is 45° 35'
Measure also the Distance CB 56 yards Take 19° 30'
out of 90° the here remaining 70° 30' for the ang AA

Detail taken from Tunis Smith's exercise book,
which shows the solution to a problem in geometry/surveying.
Tunis Smith, "His Book," Budke Collection, BC-76,
Rare Books and Manuscripts Division, The New York Public Library.

County, then as the first county clerk following the formation of
Rockland County in 1798, plus various offices, such as town supervisor
for Clarkstown and state assemblyman and state senator, were all clear
manifestations of his prominent position in the Clarkstown and broader
Rockland communities. This was a prominence based on respect and
ability rather than wealth. He had a middling real estate appraisal of
only £93 in the Clarkstown tax assessments of 1787.[14]

David Pye, like his neighbors, lived on a farm. He had an
extensive household with 14 people in 1790. In addition to his wife,
this number may have included unmarried children, possibly the family
of his married daughter, Sarah, workers on the farm, and four slaves.[15]
Because of his large household, he could leave much of the labor on
the farm to his sons and the slaves while he made surveys, drew up legal
documents, and participated in other aspects of community life. Spring
proved to be a particularly busy season for him as a surveyor. The
return of warm weather made it possible to take up activities abandoned
during the worst of the winter months. Pye's account of his activities
for April 28-30 and May 20-21, 1785 illustrates the number of different
surveys and drafts of deeds, etc. that could keep a trusted country
surveyor busy:

April 28, Surveyed this day for Jno. Zabriskee. At evening
sold a lott at Vendue, 5/16. Lodged at Garret Smiths.

April 29, Survey half day for A. Debaun, half day for
Mr. Zabriskee. Lodged with Alb't Smith.

April 30, Continued for Abram Debaun, half day, then
run between Jno. Gutche's, and his Brothers. Not finished.

May 20, Morning went to C. Smith's. Survey his Lanes. Rec'd
pay for the two Deeds of Alb't and Garret (Smith). Abraham De
Baun had his Lease and Release, Charge Mr. Lupton. Returned
to Crouter's, paid him in full for Chaining.[16]

(14) "Clarkstown District Tax List for 1787, Major John Smith, Collector," Budke Collection,
BC-52. David Pye's real estate holdings ranked 82nd out of 181 assessed individuals
who appear on the 1787 tax list and are listed in either the 1790 or 1800 census for Or-
ange/Rockland counties. John Rider had the highest real estate valuation, £600.
(15) *David Pye Diary. First Census.*
(16) Chaining: carrying the surveyor's chain to determine distances on a survey.

May 21, 1785, Saturday. Went to Hones Curtis, run the line and made Draft of the Lott. Charge it to Zabriskie. Called at Jacob Myers. Wrote over the Will of Hones Yurry. Gott Horse shoed. Returned Home late. A Subpinea [*sic*] for me to go to Chester as Evidence between Cheeswiks and Wayanda.[17]

These extracts make it clear that surveying was just one of the activities that kept Pye busy during the spring of 1785. He drew up deeds and wills for his neighbors — documents vital to the orderly transfer of land and property from one individual to another. He ran vendues, or auctions, to settle estates. He also drew up bills of sales for slaves for his neighbors. On April 1, 1785 he "wrote [the] bill (of) sale for Abraham Blauvelt for his negro sold to Geo. Van Nostrand[,] not paid." This was the second bill of sale for a slave drawn up by David Pye in 1785. On January 14, he had drawn a "Bill of Sale for a Negro of Geo. Van Nostrand to H. Oblenus, [£]73.2 paid."

Such bills of sale were not unusual in both old Orange and Rockland counties at the end of the 18th century. In 1790, Africans, the overwhelming majority of whom were enslaved, made up 8% of the total population of the area that would become Rockland County in 1798. By 1800, Africans accounted for nearly 10% of the population of Rockland.[18] Next to the land, these slaves were among the most valuable forms of property owned by Rockland's residents, and a clear chain of ownership through bills of sale protected the owner's rights.

The Courts

Properly drawn deeds, wills, land surveys, and bills of sales were all meant to guarantee the legal rights of the parties involved. As a justice of the peace, David Pye helped interpret and protect those rights and dispense justice through Orange County's quarterly sessions of the Court of General Sessions of the Peace. The court met alternately at New City and Goshen during the 1780s and 1790s until the separation of Rockland from Orange in 1798. The spring court session in 1785 ran from Tuesday, May 10 through Friday, May 13. Pye had already attended court for the winter session, January 21 and February 1, and

---

(17)   The subpoena was for Pye to testify in a lawsuit contesting the boundaries of the extensive Cheesecocks and Waywayanda patents.
(18)   *First Census.* "Federal Census 1800," pp. 350-355.

would attend the summer and fall court sessions as well. We don't know anything about the court cases heard by Pye in 1785, but scattered records of indictments and various cases heard by other sessions of the court during the 1790s make it clear that some of Rockland's residents managed to get into trouble 200 years ago, just as they do today.

The most serious charge, murder, was made against Jonathan Bell of Orangetown in 1798. Bell, a laborer, "not having the fear of God before his eyes but being moved and seduced by the Instigation of the Devil," struck "Prince, A Black Man of the Family of Onderdonk" of Nyack on December 16, 1797. As a result of this blow to the chest, Prince died that same day. Bell was indicted for murder August 18, 1798.[19] There is no record of the outcome of this case. The normal sentence for murder would have been death, although it is unlikely that Rockland County's white population would have treated the killing of a slave as murder.

Dramatic murder cases were unusual. Generally, sudden deaths were the result of accidents. The coroner's inquest of 1792 dealt with four sudden deaths. John Dunscomb drowned off Haverstraw. John Haring, the son of Abraham, drowned in a mill pond. James Talls[?] fell in the Hudson at the Hook and drowned. These were all accidental. The fourth case was not. Daniel Odle [Odell] died at Hook Mountain, but he was murdered by person or persons unknown. There is no reference to the identity of the murderer, or if he or she was eventually arrested and tried.[20] Most cases, however, dealt with items like the May 1800 arraignment of Jacob Rose, Jr., of Haverstraw for keeping a disorderly tavern[21] or with land and property disputes.

The courts also sat in judgment on family matters, including spousal abuse and cases of bastardy. In one of the few surviving cases of spousal abuse, Elizabeth Wygens of New Cornwall in modern Orange County accused her husband, John, of literally kicking her out of the house, threatening to kill her, and physically kicking his child, age 10 months, out the door. The surviving record does not indicate

(19) Arrest order for Jonathan Bell of Orangetown by James Edwords, Coroner, Orange County, December 19, 1797. Judgment, "The People ag. Jonathan Bell," August 18, 1798. *Historical Miscellanies*, collected and comp. George H. Budke, II, 1928, Budke Collection, BC-71, The New York Public Library. Manuscripts & Archives Division (Library Association of Rockland County, 1975), pp. 239-240.

(20) "Orange County, N.Y. Board of Supervisors Proceedings, 1723-1798," Budke Collection, BC-9, p. 303.

(21) "The People of the State of New York & Jacob Rose, Jun., May Term 1800," *Historical Miscellanies*, II, p. 233.

how the court acted in this case.[22] The Court of General Sessions also heard cases of bastardy, meant to establish the identity of the father and, hence, the financial responsibility of the father to provide for the child. Deadbeat dads are nothing new. In June 1795 the justices of the peace found that William Babcock, a laborer from Haverstraw, was the father of Hannah Conklin's bastard daughter. Hannah was a resident of Hempstead.[23] The court ordered that Babcock pay the overseers of the poor of Hempstead 1s. 6d. per week as child support plus 20s. to cover the cost of Hannah Conklin's lying-in.[24]

The concern of the court in this case of bastardy was not the moral issue of sexual misconduct outside of wedlock. Instead, it was concerned with the financial issue of who would be responsible for the care of the child. By law, each township was responsible for the care of its own residents, including the poor. Oversight for the care of the town's indigent fell on the overseers of the poor who received tax dollars to care for the local poor. In the case of Hannah Conklin and William Babcock, the mother and child lived in Hempstead while the father lived in Haverstraw, beyond the jurisdiction of the overseers of Hempstead. The county court provided a vehicle to force the father to pay child support to another town.

Churches and Religious Observations

While the courts concerned themselves with issues of financial responsibility, the church played the major role in monitoring the morals of the community. Rockland County residents could choose between several different churches by the end of the 18th century. The decision to attend a particular church was as likely to rest on practical considerations of location and language of the worship service as it was to indicate denominational preferences. David Pye, for example, attended both the nearby Dutch Reformed Church of Clarkstown and the more distant New Hempstead Presbyterian Church, also known as the English Meeting House at Kakiat. He did not attend church every Sunday. Sometimes he remained at home because of the weather, such as on April 3, 1785: "Stormy and bad Traveling. Staid this day in the

(22) Court of General Sessions of the Peace, October 3, 1792, Budke Collection, BC-77.
(23) In 1795 Hannah's town would have been called "New Hempstead." The "New" was dropped in 1797.
(24) "The Overseers of the Poor for the Town of New Hempstead vs. William Babcock: Order in Bastardy," June 26, 1795, Budke Collection, BC-35.

The Tappan Dutch Reformed Church

Built in 1716

Built in 1788

Built in 1835

In 1716 the congregation of the Tappan Reformed Church replaced their original log cabin house of worship with a stone structure. Here, during the American Revolution, British Major John André was tried and convicted as a spy. Later, in 1788, the building was enlarged and the four-sided roof was replaced by a gambrel roof.

From Cole, *History of Rockland County, New York.*

House." On other occasions he chose to remain at home for unknown reasons: "June 5 [1785], Sabboth. This day Stayd in the House." David Pye seldom commented on the sermons he heard, except to identify which church he attended and who preached that day. The Dominie Nicholas Lansing served as minister to both the Tappan Dutch Reformed Church and the Clarkstown Dutch Reformed Church. Originally Dominie Lansing preached in Dutch, but the growth of the English-speaking population made it necessary for him to preach in English as well as Dutch after the Revolution. In his diary, David Pye reported that "Mr. Lansing preached in English" on May 22 and on several other occasions.[25] It is not clear if Dominie Lansing alternated his sermons, one week preaching in English and the next in Dutch, or if David Pye attended the Clarkstown church only when Dominie Lansing preached in English. The Clarkstown congregation was largely English speaking, making the need for English sermons much more apparent here than at the older Tappan church. The Tappan congregation had a larger Dutch-speaking contingent, and Dutch remained the preferred language, although Dominie Lansing also alternated between Dutch and English in Tappan by the turn of the century.[26]

Although David Pye frequently attended the Dutch Reformed Church, he was elected trustee of the New Hempstead Presbyterian Church in 1785, becoming a member of that church in 1790. Organized by 1734, the Kakiat Presbyterian congregation had built its meeting house by 1754.[27] The Kakiat church appears to have offered more variety in its preaching than the sermons given by Dominie Lansing. During June 1785, David Pye attended the Kakiat meeting three times. On one occasion he heard a Mr. Bradner preach, and on the other two occasions Mr. Carr preached.[28] It was common for traveling ministers to speak at different churches each Sunday, particularly when a preacher's pastoral responsibilities covered a large geographic area. Local members might preach when the minister was at a different location.

---

(25) David Pye Diary, January 9, July 17, & November 6, 1785.

(26) See Cole, History of Rockland County, pp. 232-237 for a brief biography of Nicholas Lansing and his work in the Tappan and Clarkstown churches.

(27) See "Historical Sketch: The New Hempstead Presbyterian Church," address by Charles C. Husson, delivered at 200th Anniversary Celebration, Two Hundredth Anniversary Celebration, New Hempstead Presbyterian Church, New Hempstead, N.Y., October 19 to 21, 1934 and New Hempstead Presbyterian Church: A History of the Old English Meeting House, New Hempstead Presbyterian Church, 1987.

(28) David Pye Diary, June 12, June 19, & June 26, 1785.

David Pye alternated between the two most centrally located churches, the Dutch Reformed Church at Clarkstown and the English Presbyterian Church at Kakiat. The residents in the southern part of the county had long found the Tappan Dutch Reformed Church most convenient. Residents in the northern reaches of the county waited the longest for the establishment of nearby churches. In 1774 the Dutch Reformed Church expanded north and west of Clarkstown to form the West New Hempstead Dutch Reformed Church. Its congregation constructed a small, wooden structure that served both as a school and church in 1778. Those northernmost residents who preferred an English service waited until 1789 before they had a local church. At that time the Haverstraw Presbyterian Church was built.

These five churches, three Dutch Reformed and two Presbyterian, comprised the formal congregations in existence in Rockland right up until the end of the century. Then, in 1798 and 1799 two new churches appeared. The Rockland Baptist Church (today's Grace Conservative Baptist Church in Nanuet) was formed in 1798, although it met at the homes of members until the 19th century. It was very small in these early years with only 12 members along the New York-New Jersey border. The next year, a Methodist Society was formed in Haverstraw with a building erected in 1800.[29] The Baptists and the Methodists would have a major impact on the growth of churches in the 18th century but played a minor role in Rockland in the 1790s.[30]

Tunis Smith, living in Nyack, attended the Tappan Dutch Reformed Church. In his "Remembrance," Tunis recounts his marriage to Mary Smith at Tappan on August 22, 1794. Dominie Lansing officiated at the ceremony.[31] We don't know if Smith attended with any greater regularity than David Pye, but he kept track of at least some of the Dutch religious holidays. Smith noted that he bought his four-year-old stallion on April the 17th, 1793, "Pingster."[32] Pinkster is the

---

(29) Records in the possession of the Thiells United Methodist Church indicate that John Wesley authorized a Methodist mission in the Thiells area to serve the local Indians in 1784. It is unclear, however, how active this group was as a congregation for the local, non-Indian population. Daniel deNoyelles, *Thiells United Methodist Church Bicentennial, 1784-1984*, pp. 2-3.

(30) Frank Bertangue Green, M.D., *The History of Rockland County, New York* (1886; reprint ed., New City, N.Y.: The Historical Society of Rockland County, 1989), pp. 222-277, provides an overview of the history of all the principal churches in Rockland into the 1880s.

(31) p. 52.

(32) p. 50. Pinkster follows 50 days after Easter. As a result it does not have a fixed date but can fall anywhere from mid-April through the end of May or early June, depending on the church calendar.

Dutch term for the celebration of Pentecost, called Whitsunday in the English tradition. David Pye, with his English background, referred to May 15, 1785 as "Sabbath. Whitsontide." Pinkster, as a holiday, was associated specifically with those areas of New York and northern New Jersey that retained a distinctly Dutch character late in the 18th century. That Dutch association took Pinkster beyond the purely religious celebration as practiced in the various Christian churches and gave it a distinctly festive, secular character, one readily assimilated and eventually taken over by the African community, both free and enslaved.

> June 4, 1786
> It is all frolicing to-day with the Dutch and the Negro. This is a holy day, Whitsunday, called among the Dutch "Pinkster," and they have eggs boiled in all sorts of colors, and eggs cooked in every way, and everybody must eat all the eggs he can. And the frolicing is still kept up among the young folk, so that little else is done to-day but eat eggs and be jolly.
> ...Wm Coventry took the girls over to Legat's for a frolic.
>
> June 5   Alexander sleeping today, being tired with frolicing yesterday and last night.
>
> June 6   Still frolicing Dutch Pinkster.
>
> June 1, 1789
> Cuff [a slave] keeping Pinkster, a festival or feast among the Dutch. (Monday).[33]

As a newly arrived Scotsman who had recently settled in the Claverack area, Alexander Coventry found the Pinkster celebrations of his neighbors noteworthy. They seemed to be unique to areas with a continued strong Dutch presence. Similar celebrations occurred in the Dutch areas of New Jersey. William Dunlap toured through Passaic in 1797 and remarked on the festive spirit among the Dutch and Africans he encountered:

---

(33)   Coventry, "Memoirs of an Emigrant," 1:108, 215.

June 6, 1797

The settlements along the river are dutch, it is the holiday
they call pinkster & every public house is crowded with
merry makers & waggon's full of rustic beaux & belles
met us at every mile. The blacks as well as their masters
were frolicking and the women & children look'd peculiarly neat and well dressed.[34]

Later references carry the tradition of Pinkster into the 19th
century, but with an increasingly African, rather than Dutch association. It continued to be celebrated in areas that had been associated with
the Dutch, especially on Long Island and around Albany, during the
first half of the 19th century, then gradually vanished from view.

Pinkster frolics were unique to the spring, but frolics could occur
at any time. Daniel Martine, of Orangetown, invited his neighbors to
a frolic on June 18, 1785. David Pye does not tell us the reason for the
frolic, but he attended after picking up some things at Nyack that had
just arrived from New York. These frolics were parties, frequently a
work party in that the guests helped out on a project, then had a party
to celebrate the completion of the job. Quilting frolics, corn shucking
frolics, and other activities provided an excuse for neighbors to get
together, gossip, drink, eat, dance, and generally break up the monotony
of life on isolated farmsteads. Mid- to late June would have been a
good time to take a break. The majority of the crops had been ploughed
and sown. Soon it would be time to begin the haying and the summer
harvests.

Summer:
July, August, and September

In this season, as well as in the spring, the farmer has
plenty of work. Crops that are to be hoed, are first to be
attended to, and must by no means be neglected. There is
often much of this work to do in a little time, especially
on farms where much Indian corn is raised. And the more

---

(34) *Diary of William Dunlap (1766-1839): The Memoirs of a Dramatist, Theatrical Man-
      ager, Painter, Critic, Novelist, and Historian,* Collections of The New-York Historical
      Society for the Year 1930, 3 vols. in 1 (reprint ed., New York: Benjamin Blom, 1969),
      p. 65.

fruitful the season is, the more frequently hoeings will be needful, to keep the weeds under. This work can hardly be, and seldom is finished, before the grass on the highlands calls for mowing. And before the mowing season is ended, reaping, and the toil of the former harvest, come on.

The summer business is more toilsome, on account of the intense heat of a considerable part of that season. To lighten the labours of the fields, the farmer and his men should be at their work early and late, and rest themselves during the hottest hours. Thus they may perform as much as they ought to do, without fatiguing or overheating themselves, and without exciting such an immoderate thirst as will tempt them to ruin their constitutions with cold drinks.[35]

Spring ran into summer with little abatement in tasks to be performed. The spring planting season merged with the summer mowing and harvesting season. In addition, the kitchen garden required constant attention to take full advantage of the fruit and vegetables as they ripened. They could be eaten fresh, but most importantly they could be dried, pickled, or turned into jams or jellies to provide variety for the long winter months ahead. These jobs usually fell to the women of the household while the men concentrated on the fields and pastures.

Field Crops

Tunis Smith remembered starting the long summer months of 1793 with the winter wheat and rye harvest. "We begun in our Harvest on a thurday [sic] afternoon and got Done with the Rye on thuesday [sic] the 8th[.] We had 34 wagon Load of it. And finished with the Wheat, and Sowing Bucwheat [sic] that week."[36] David Pye began July 1785 ploughing the potatoes (July 1) and harrowing the ground in one of his fields (July 5). He planted his buckwheat in mid-July (July 15), possibly an indication that spring came earlier in 1793 than it had in 1785. But the big activity for mid-July was mowing and haying. David's son John began mowing grass on July 13. David and his entire

(35) Deane, *Georgical Dictionary*, p. 328.
(36) Tunis Smith, "Remembrance," p. 51.

Harvest scene, woodcut by Alexander Anderson.
Print Collection, Miriam and Ira D. Wallach Division of Art, Prints, and
Photographs, The New York Public Library, Astor, Lenox, and Tilden Foundations.

household, sons and slaves, returned to the hay fields on the 14th and
the 15th. They kept the Sabbath on the 17th, with Dominie Lansing
preaching in English at the Clarkstown church, but returned to the fields
on Monday, Tuesday, and Wednesday, the 20th. The weather played
a critical role in haying. The hay had to be completely dry before it
could be stacked or put in a barrack. Summer showers and thunder-
storms constantly threatened to destroy the hay crop once it was lying
in the field. David Pye and his family were evidently lucky in 1785.
They finished the hay crop on July 20. On July 21 it rained. Three days
later, on the 24th, David Pye made his last entry until October 1, 1785.
He doesn't say why he stopped keeping the diary for this two-month
period, but the next two months would have been the busiest part of the
harvest.

     The crops raised by Rockland's farmers in the 18th century ran
to a few tried and true staples, with little variety. These crops had to
be ploughed or hoed or weeded, mowed, harvested, carted, stacked,
cleaned and prepared for the mill. Few things could stop the momentum of the season, once started. Everything had to be taken care of

when it was ripe, before it rained, before it could spoil. The activity seldom stopped.

But it could stop. It stopped on Bridget Vanderbilt's Clarkstown farm on August 2, 1798. It stopped on Rebecca and Harmanus Tallman's Nyack farm on August 20, 1798. Death stopped the farming activity, if only for the length of time it took for appraisers to come in and inventory the farm, house, and personal possessions of the deceased.

When Bridget Vanderbilt died, much of the work of the summer had yet to be accomplished. She had sown buckwheat. It remained in the field. Wheat and rye had been scythed and the sheaves bundled together, but they had not yet been threshed. The oats needed to be harvested. Potatoes continued to ripen in the ground, and the corn grew in hillocks. Her grass and hay had been mowed and possibly stacked. Her flax had been pulled but was not yet dressed. The peaches and apples remained on the trees in the orchard.[37]

Two-and-a-half weeks later, the situation on the Tallman farm was a little more advanced when David Pye and Michael Cornelison, Jr., went to appraise the property. The hay had been mowed, turned, carted out of the fields, and stored in the loft and in two lean-tos attached to the barn. The rye crop had been good, with more than 1,700 sheaves stored away until they could be threshed. There were still four-and-a-half acres of corn and potatoes in the ground, and four-and-a-half acres of buckwheat sown in the field. Next year's winter wheat would be sown at the end of the summer, and two bushels of "sowing wheat" had been set aside for that purpose. A half bushel of rye awaited fall planting. Like Bridget Vanderbilt, the Tallmans had undressed flax waiting to be cleaned. In addition they had a small turnip yard and a small patch of broom corn.[38]

The two bushels of "sowing wheat" set aside for the late summer planting at the Tallman farm had little chance of producing a successful crop the following year. Winter wheat, wheat planted in the fall and harvested early the following summer, had long been a staple crop on farms in the Hudson River Valley. The local farmers grew red lammas. "The best wheat for Sowing is the Red Lammas wheat red in the Stalk

(37) Inventory of the Estate of Bridget Vanderbilt, Widow, August, 2, 1798, Surrogate's Court, Rockland County, New City.
(38) Inventory of the Estate of Harmanus Tallman, August 20, 1798, Surrogate's Court, Rockland County.

Ear & Skin of the Grain, but...Whitest of all the flour, this is the reason that Farmers prefer the Red Lammas wheat to all other kinds."[39] But the days when Hudson Valley wheat fields flourished had ended by the 1790s. The Hessian fly, a small insect that arrived in this country with the British army during the Revolution, had refused to leave when the British withdrew from New York in 1783. Instead it ravished the wheat crops each year until by the 1790s most farmers had ceased planting wheat entirely, resorting to rye and corn as alternative cash crops. Travelers on both sides of the Hudson remarked on the decline of the wheat crop by the end of the 18th century. William Strickland visited Westchester in the fall of 1794 and saw little wheat in an area where it had once flourished.

> Much wheat used to be grown in this neighbourhood, but the Hessian fly has stopped the cultivation; no wheat can resist its attack, except the white bearded wheat, which is of inferior quality; in the place of it they sow rye and plant corn. This insect attacks the root and stalk in the spring when the plant is about two feet high — and sometimes at a later period; after which the plant dies.[40]

Henry Wansey, a visiting British industrialist, traveled through Newark, New Jersey and saw similar depredations by the fly and the resulting shift in crops. "They cultivate little or no wheat in these parts, on account of the Hessian fly, rye and oats are the chief produce of the country."[41] The farmers of Rockland, like their neighbors in Westchester and New Jersey, also gave up on wheat as a viable cash crop. Despite its presence in both the Vanderbilt and Tallman inventories, wheat could no longer be relied upon to produce a cash crop. In its place Rocklanders began planting oats to feed New York City's horses and also rye and corn.

The Tallmans' "sowing wheat" would have been sown in September along with the next year's rye crop. If it had been a good year with an early spring, the farmers might be fortunate enough to get in a

(39)   Verplanck Farm Book, Dutchess County, ca. 1790, The New-York Historical Society, New York, typescript, p. 74.
(40)   *Journal of a Tour*, October 6, 1794, p. 90.
(41)   *Henry Wansey and His American Journal*, June 4, 1794, p. 91.

The estate inventory of Bridget Vanderbilt, made August 2, 1798, includes a large variety of farm implements, crops, and "sundries," including parcels of wheat, buckwheat, "Brand," and corn.
Rockland County Surrogate's Court, New City, New York.
Photo by Jeffrey Hunter.

second cutting of hay. By the end of September, the sowing for the year was just about completed, but the final harvesting remained. Corn had to be topped, and the first pickings could be made by the end of September. The fruit in the orchard had ripened. Early apples and pears were ready to be picked. The fruit could be eaten raw, cooked in pies and tarts, made into jelly, or pressed for a beverage. A surplus of apples and pears meant cash from the New York City market.

Farmers and their families could not limit their activities to field crops. Wives and daughters still concentrated on preserving the fruits and vegetables of the kitchen garden, the orchard, and the fields and meadows. Berries were seldom planted in kitchen gardens because they grew wild in abundance in the woods and fields. Peas and beans from the garden were dried. As the fruit from the orchard ripened, it too was prepared for drying. Apples, pears, and peaches could all be sliced thin and laid out in the sun to dry or be placed in a warm beehive oven for several hours until all the moisture in the fruit had evaporated. Then it could be strung together and hung in the attic or a dry cellar. Later, in the winter, the fruit would be soaked in water and used in baking.

In addition to the grains, potatoes, and turnips that filled the narrow farm fields, Rockland's farmers also planted small fields of flax, the fiber from which linen is made. It was pulled from the ground in the summer rather than cut. This way, the long flax fibers that run the complete length of the stalk, from root to tip, would not be shortened. Once pulled from the fields, the flax had to be retted, that is, placed in pools of water so that the outer sheaf of the plant would rot away, leaving the long flax fibers that would be separated from the sheaf, cleaned, and eventually spun into thread.[42] Henry Eslor, who died in the spring of 1799, had 71 bundles of flax still waiting to be processed so it could be spun into thread.[43] Both Jonah Halstead and Harmanus Tallman owned flax hetchels, tools used to clean and straighten the flax fiber before it is spun.[44]

Indian corn was treated somewhat differently from the rest of the field crops. Wheat, rye, oats, and buckwheat were all sown broadcast and then allowed to grow on their own. They were seldom weeded and

---

(42)   Thread refers to linen thread, sometimes cotton. Yarn refers to spun wool.
(43)   Inventory of Henry J. Eslor, Hempstead, April 22, 1799, Surrogate's Court, Rockland County.
(44)   Inventory of Jonah Halstead, Hempstead, January 29, 1800, Surrogate's Court, Rockland County.

Threshing scene, woodcut by Alexander Anderson. Using flails, the wheat berry is beaten off the stem. The wheat is then winnowed by tossing it into the air where the heavy wheat berries fall back into the winnowing tray and the lighter chaff blows away.
Print Collection, Miriam and Ira D. Wallach Division of Art, Prints, and Photographs, The New York Public Library, Astor, Lenox, and Tilden Foundations.

grew unevenly over the field. Corn, on the other hand, was planted in clusters of three to four kernels, each cluster separated from the next by roughly five feet in all directions. This allowed the farmer to cross plough between the clusters while the plant was small, pushing up a small hill of dirt around each cluster of stalks. Over the summer the hillocks created by the plough had to be hoed by hand to control the weeds. This was a time-consuming operation, particularly when the hay had to be mowed and stacked and the wheat and rye needed to be scythed and gathered during the same period. Other crops could be planted around the corn. Squash and pumpkin vines climbed the stalks, or rye could be planted between the stalks, leaving a field of rye once the corn had been harvested.

Fourth of July

The summer, like the spring, was among the busiest seasons for the farmer, but he rested on the Sabbath, attending church and visiting with neighbors whenever possible. Everyone paused, at least for a short time, on the Fourth of July to celebrate the first national holiday. David Pye's account of Monday, July 4, 1785 seemed to describe a day like any other, except at the very end: "Prest Cloth & the last that I had ready. Th. Thew at Copper this day. T. James working for Samy. Independence. 13 Crackers, etc."

The 13 crackers that ended the Fourth of July for David Pye typified the celebration full of noise and picnics that has marked the nation's birthday since the end of the 18th century. William Dunlap described the Fourth in New York City as "A day of Noise & parade."[45] It was, in fact, a holiday that blended the public with the private, according to the interests of the local community. Henry Wansey, stopping in Newark in June, listened to a discussion on how that town's inhabitants would celebrate the upcoming Fourth. The community decided to have a public commemoration but leave any decisions about parties and other festivities to the individual.

> June 12, 1794
> Hearing there was a meeting of the inhabitants, I followed the crowd into a large town hall, where I found them debating about the means and ordering of the commemoration of July 4, then approaching, (the aera [sic] of their independence.) It was determined there should be a procession to church, and a sermon preached on the occasion, but as to a feast, it was decreed, that every person should do as they liked best.[46]

The residents of Rockland undoubtedly followed a similar pattern, although the public orations became more and more important as the turn of the century approached.

By 1800 the Fourth of July had become the natural occasion for newly formed political parties to expound on their patriotism. In urban centers and small villages the town's principal citizens, residents, and local politicians met at the local taverns to toast the nation's leaders and the Revolution. In rural areas throughout the nation, the local militia paraded, the minister preached a patriotic sermon, and families and friends gathered together for picnics and small parties. There are no surviving descriptions of these early Fourth of July celebrations in Rockland itself, but those from other areas are probably quite repre-

(45) *Diary of William Dunlap*, July 4, 1797, p. 93.
(46) *Henry Wansey and His American Journal*, p. 126.

sentative. When J.B. Dunlop left Albany for central New York on July 4, 1811, he encountered a countryside intent on relaxation and festivities:

> Although we were determined to retire from the bustle of the city early in the morning we were not able to get away until the afternoon, not being able to prevail on any one of the drivers to leave a scene which was so pleasant to them, and as we traveled along we perceived groups of country people feasting under the trees in every direction, in celebration of this momentous era....

The more settled the area, the more elaborate the festivities. Before Dunlop encountered the country folk picnicking under the trees, he had been awakened to a much more vocal celebration in Albany proper:

> The discharge of cannon soon after we got to bed ushered in the morning of the 4 July, a day regarded by all the Americans with the utmost veneration and celebrated with a frenzy approaching to madness by the Democratic party. The military assemble and after performing a few revolutions retire to one of the most commodious churches, where one of the young graduates, previously appointed, delivers an oration, upon which his success or insignificancy as a lawyer generally depends. The pulpit from whence the word of God is communicated to men is now converted into a forum from whence [with] the most sacrilegious curses and profane epithets[,] are denounced all the would be enemies of America. The oration finished, Democrat & Federal join their different and distinct parties; and [the] former spends the remainder of the day in one of the inns, opposite to which the Cap of Liberty is erected on a pole, where they indulge in all the irregularities of licentious liberty; the latter retire to their families where among their friends they celebrate with moderation the anniversary of that day which secured to them the right of independence.

Dunlop's trip, delayed by the celebrations in Albany, was cut short that night in Schenectady, where he witnessed the noisy and spectacular finale to the day in a fireworks display over the Mohawk River.

> We arrived at Schenectady, a beautiful little city situated on the banks of the Mohawk River, in time to witness a magnificent spectacle, which was displayed in commemoration of the evening. There was a grand display of fire works on the Mohawk river, the banks of which, as well as the beautiful bridge over it, were crowded with people, whilst innumerable boats, filled with the genteel class, moved upon the smooth surface of the river to the reverberating echo of a band of music which filled up the intervals between each fire rocket with martial music.[47]

David Pye's "13 Crackers" may have seemed small compared to these elaborate public demonstrations of patriotism displayed in Albany and Schenectady, but he and his fellow Rocklanders took time to remember the Fourth, even in the midst of all the summer hoeing, mowing, and harvesting.

The Hessian Fly

---

(47)   "From the Windows of the Mail Coach," pp. 275-276. As should be obvious from the above quotation, Dunlop favored the more restrained, conservative approach to celebration manifested by members of the Federal Party.

Fall:
October, November, and December

> ...In this quarter of the year, the farmer finishes his harvesting, and lays in his stores for the winter.
>
> In a country where the springs are backward..., farmers should do all they can in autumn, to diminish or lighten the labours of the following spring, when they will have much work to perform in a short time. Summer dung and composts should be carted out at this season. Fences should be built or repaired, not only to prevent having them to do in the spring, but to keep cattle from injuring the lands with their feet. All the ground should be ploughed in the fall that is to be seeded the following spring. That which is intended for spring wheat should be ploughed twice. Though all that is ploughed in the fall, for spring tillage, must be ploughed again before seeding, the fall ploughing saves labour, as one ploughing may answer in the spring where two would be otherwise needful. It is saving labour at a time when teams are most apt to be faint and feeble, and when there is too often a scarcity of food for them. But ploughing in autumn is of great importance in a clay soil, as, by exposing it to the frost the cohesion of its parts is much broken.
>
> The transplanting of trees out of nurseries may, to redeem time, be performed in the fall; though, on other accounts, I should prefer doing it in the spring.[48]

As the *Georgical Dictionary* makes clear, the fall months were spent finishing the tasks associated with summer, especially the harvesting of corn, buckwheat, potatoes, and apples and making the final preparations for the winter months. David Pye's men completed the buckwheat harvest in mid-October. They thrashed and cleaned the buckwheat on the 27th through the 29th. By November 4 they had begun bringing in the corn. The buckwheat went to the miller's on the 10th. The potatoes still needed to be dug out and stacked, an operation

---

(48)   Deane, *Georgical Dictionary*, p. 101.

that began on the 11th.[49] For Tunis Smith, in 1793, the harvest began earlier. He and his father "mow'd" the buckwheat beginning September 18 and threshed it out on October 7.[50]

The corn, or maize, required special attention. Unlike the other grains that could be threshed with a flail and cleaned with a winnowing tray, the corn had to be shucked by hand and the outer husk removed as soon as possible so that it would not rot and destroy the kernels on the ear. This was a big, time-consuming job, more readily accomplished by large numbers of people working together. It also had to be done shortly after the crop was picked. It was a natural opportunity for a work party: a husking frolic. Mme. de la Tour du Pin described such a husking party at her farm in 1795:

> The apple picking was followed by the harvesting of the maize. We had an abundance of it, for it is indigenous to the United States and grows there better than any other plant. As the corn must not be left in the husk for more than two days, the neighbours collect to help, and they work without stopping until it is all done. This is called a "frolic." First, the floor of the barn is swept with as much care as for a ball. Then, when darkness comes, candles are lit and the people assemble, about thirty of them, both black and white, and they set to work. All night long someone sings or tells stories and in the middle of the night everyone is given a bowl of boiling milk, previously turned with cider, to which have been added cloves, cinnamon, nutmeg and other spices, and five or six pounds of brown sugar, if one is being very grand, or a similar quantity of molasses if one feels less grand. We prepared a kitchen boiler full of this mixture and our workers paid us the compliment of drinking it all, eating toast which accompanied it. These good people left us at five o'clock in the morning, going out into the sharp cold, saying "Famous good people, those from the old country!" Our negroes were often asked to similar frolics, but my negress never went.[51]

(49) David Pye Diary, passim.
(50) Tunis Smith, "Remembrance," p. 52.
(51) Memoirs of Madame de la Tour du Pin, p. 278.

Although Mme. de la Tour du Pin lived in the Mohawk Valley, similar frolics would have been held at Rockland farms during the chilly November days and nights.

Apples and Cider

Mme. de la Tour du Pin also mentioned the apple harvest that she had completed before her husking frolic. Apples flourished throughout New York, and farms almost always included an orchard. Alexander Coventry, seeing the scattered farms of southern Rockland from across the river, thought the small orchards that surrounded even the meanest of huts rendered "them agreeable to the eye."[52]pples, in particular, were vitally important to the farm families in Rockland and throughout New York. Edward Dixon, a newly arrived Englishman intent on settling across the Hudson in Westchester County, wrote back to England about the people and customs of his new homeland. He found apples grown everywhere. Each farm had "apples amazingly plentiful, some have orchards of 1, some 10, some twenty acres, that afford them Cyder and Apples to sell and keep to themselves untill a fresh supply come again. I have seen I'm sure 20 or 25 Bushels often upon one Tree...."[53]

> ...near every farm-house [in New York] was an orchard with apple trees. Here, and on the whole journey before, I observed a press for cyder at every farm-house, made in different manners, by which the people had already pressed the juice out of the apples, or were just busied with that work. Some people made use of a wheel made of thick oak planks, which turned upon a wooden axis, by means of a horse drawing it, much in the same manner as the people do with woad; except that here the wheel runs upon planks.[54]

---

(52)   "Memoirs of an Emigrant," p. 70.
(53)   Edward Dixon to George Dixon, December 23, 1800, Ossining Historical Society, Ossining, New York.
(54)   Peter Kalm, *Travels into North America*, October 30, 1748, p. 124.

Mme. de la Tour du Pin described a slightly different cider press on her farm in 1795:

> We were lent a mill for pressing the apples and to it we harnessed an ancient, twenty-three-year-old horse which General Schuyler had given me. The mill was exceedingly primitive: there were two interlocking, grooved pieces of wood, like ratchets, and these were turned by the horse, which was harnessed to a wooden bar. The apples fell from a hopper into the interlocking pieces of wood and when there was enough juice to fill a large basket, it was taken to the cellar and poured into the casks.
>
> The whole operation was exceedingly simple and as the weather was very fine, this harvesting became a delightful recreation for us.[55]

The cider produced by these primitive but effective presses was stored in kegs, allowed to ferment over the winter, and was ready to drink during the heat of the next summer. Sweet cider, that taken directly from the presses, could be enjoyed in the fall and was a favorite with children and adults alike. However, the bulk of the cider was hard. The alcohol acted as a natural preservative, allowing each year's harvest to be saved for the next year.

The apples that were not pressed for cider could be cut, dried, and hung in the attic or dairy room for later use. The very best apples, those without blemish, would be carefully placed in barrels, surrounded by straw, and set aside to be eaten throughout the winter and spring months. As early as 1750 apples had become a trademark of hospitality among the farmers in New York:

> It was a common custom in the English colonies, when anyone paid a visit to a house, to bring in a large dish of apples and invite the guests to partake of them. In the evening when we sat warming ourselves before the fire,

---

(55) *Memoirs of Madame de la Tour du Pin*, pp. 277-278.

a basket of apples was carried in and all in the house ate them according to their desire.[56]

Apples also had a ready market in New York City. Any excess fruit could be carted to Tappan Slote, Nyack, or Haverstraw, loaded on to a market sloop or periauger, and sent to New York City. The farmer might be paid in cash. Or he might prefer to get the value of the apples in various manufactured goods such as textiles and hardware that were difficult to find in Rockland itself. Rockland residents like Bridget Vanderbilt, with her apple and peach orchard, and Henry J. Eslor, with his 36 apple trees, would have been in a good position to take advantage of this New York City market.[57]

Livestock

Once the crops had been taken care of, farmers made the important decision of which livestock would be wintered over and which would be slaughtered in late November and December. The size of the herd or flock that was kept through the winter months depended on the size of the summer and fall harvest. If it had been a poor year, there would be relatively little fodder for the animals during the winter months. Only the best milkers, the most prolific and healthy of the ewes, and the strongest oxen would be kept. The others would either be sold to drovers to be driven to the New York City slaughterhouses, or they would be slaughtered by the farmer himself, the meat smoked, salted, or dried for later consumption during the winter and spring.

David Pye slaughtered his cattle and pigs in the falls of 1784 and 1785. On November 29, 1785 he wrote in his diary, "Fetched Cow from Doctor's and killed her." On December 3, 1784 he "Killed Hoggs." On the 14th he retrieved a cow and a steer that he had been pasturing at a neighbor's, then butchered the cow on the 15th, despite the fact that she was carrying a calf. On December 28, 1785 he butchered a steer.

(56)   Peter Kalm, *The America of 1750: Peter Kalm's Travels in North America, The English Version of 1770*, ed. Adolph B. Benson, 2 vols. (1937; reprint ed., New York: Dover Publications, 1964), October 28, 1749, p. 604.
(57)   Inventory of Bridget Vanderbilt, August 2, 1798; Inventory of Henry J. Eslor, April 22, 1799, Surrogate's Court, Rockland County.

As a rule, hogs were kept strictly as food stock, while cattle provided muscle to pull the plough and cart as well as milk, butter, and meat for the table. Pork was probably the most commonly eaten meat, usually salted and smoked as ham and bacon or preserved as heavily spiced sausages. Cattle were not raised for their meat, and as a result the beef that was available was usually stringy and tough, coming from old cows and oxen that were no longer productive. Without refrigeration, meat spoiled quickly. Fresh meat in general was available only in the cold winter months, when the flesh could be kept fresh for a short period of time. The rest of the year Rockland's farmers subsisted on salted, dried, or smoked meats, supplemented by fish from the river and wild game, especially pigeons in the spring and fall.

Pigeons

The semiannual flights of the passenger pigeon each spring and fall provided the tables of Rockland with a favored dish. The migrations of these colorful, and decidedly edible, birds brought a welcome change to the standard farm diet. You did not even need a gun to get the birds, which were not known for their intelligence, just for their abundance. J. Hector St. John de Crèvecoeur described the flights over Chester and the technique used by local farmers to fill their nets with this succulent treat:

> We have twice a year the pleasure of catching pigeons, whose numbers are sometimes so astonishing as to obscure the sun in their flight....We catch them with a net extended on the ground, to which they are allured by what we call *tame wild pigeons*, made blind, and fastened to a long string; his short flights, and his repeated calls, never fail to bring them down. The greatest number I ever catched was fourteen dozen, though much larger quantities have often been trapped....Every farmer has a tame wild pigeon in a cage at his door all the year round, in order to be ready whenever the season comes for catching them.[58]

(58)   J. Hector St. John Crèvecoeur, *Letters from an American Farmer*, reprint based on 1782 original (Gloucester, Mass.: Peter Smith, 1968), p. 38.

To roast Pigeons.

FILL them with parsley, clean washed and chopped, and some pepper and salt rolled in butter; fill the bellies, tie the neck-end close, so that nothing can run out; put a skewer through the legs, and have a little iron on purpose, with fix hooks to it, and on each hook hang a pigeon; fasten one end of the string to the chimney, and the other end to the iron (this is what we call the poor man's spit); flour them, baste them with butter, and turn them gently for fear of hitting the bars. They will roast nicely, and be full of gravy. Take care how you take them off, not to lose any of the liquor. You may melt a very little butter, and put into the dish. Your pigeons ought to be quite fresh, and not too much done. This is by much the best way of doing them, for then they will swim in their own gravy, and a very little melted butter will do.

N.B. You may spit them on a long small spit, only tie both ends close; and send parsley and butter in one boat and gravy in another.

When you roast them on a spit, all the gravy runs out; or if you stuff them and broil them whole, you cannot save the gravy well; though they will be very good with parsley and butter in the dish; or split and broiled, with pepper and salt.

The recipe "To roast Pigeons" shows just one of the many ways in which Rockland County reisdents could prepare the native passenger pigeons that flew over the area twice each year. Hannah Glasse, *The Art of Cookery Made Plain and Easy*, London, originally published anonymously by "A Lady" in 1756, was issued under Hannah Glasse in 1796.

Collections of Historic Hudson Valley, Tarrytown, New York.
Recipe transcribed with permission.

Bridget Vanderbilt owned just such a pigeon net when she died in 1798. Henry J. Eslor of Hempstead had both a pigeon net and a pigeon cage for his "tame wild pigeon."[59]

The sheer numbers of pigeons captured and killed each season was overwhelming. Their arrival marked another welcome break from the monotony of everyday farm life, one that Anne Grant described as "a total relaxation from all employments, and a kind of drunken gaiety, though it was rather slaughter than sport; and, for above a fortnight, pigeons in pies and soups, and every way they could be dressed, were the food of the inhabitants."[60]

---

(59) Inventory of Bridget Vanderbilt; Inventory of Henry J. Eslor, Surrogate's Court, Rockland County.
(60) *Memoirs of an American Lady, with Sketches of Manners and Scenes in America as they existed previous to the Revolution*, 2 vols. (London: 1808; reprint ed., New York: Research Reprints, 1970), pp. 69-70.

Sheep and Wool

While Rockland's farmers busied themselves with the final harvest and trimmed back the livestock in preparation for the cold, winter months, their wives and daughters sometimes found the time to spin their flax fibers into thread and their wool into yarn. The sheep that grazed on the Rockland hillsides were kept primarily for their wool. Mutton was not a favored meat in New York. The small flocks that roamed Rockland's rugged hills and valleys were expected to provide wool for clothing, not food for the table.

Some, but not all, of Rockland farms raised sheep along with the more common cattle, horses, swine, and fowl, but the flocks were quite modest. Of 11 estate inventories made between 1798 and 1800, four listed sheep. Jonah Halstead of Hempstead owned a flock of eight sheep. Arthur Paul of Clarkstown kept nine sheep.[61] Bridget Vanderbilt had the largest flock with 13 sheep, plus a dog that probably worked as a shepherd. Henry J. Eslor's Hempstead flock was much smaller, only three sheep. These sheep, like their counterparts throughout the Hudson Valley, were generally undistinguished. Major improvements in the breeds of sheep would be made in the early 1800s, but in the 1780s and 1790s, the sheep had small, bony carcasses and a light, stringy fleece. As with all livestock, the quality of sheep could vary considerably from flock to flock. William Strickland seemed to like the flock he saw in Mt. Pleasant in October 1794, remarking that

> ...the sheep much resemble the Cheviot breed; some have horns, and generally grey faces and legs; their carcasses are good, their head fine, neck and legs, longish they may weigh about 16 lbs: a Quarter and are upon the whole a good breed; they produce about 3 lbs: of wool each, which is of a good staple, measuring 4 or 5 Inches, but in general coarse and harsh, selling for about 2/6 pr: lb:.[62]

Two days later, he passed through Poughkeepsie and saw a flock of a totally different character:

---

(61) Inventory of Jonah Halstead, January 29, 1800; Inventory of Arthur Paul, December 17, 1800, Surrogate's Court, Rockland County.

(62) *Journal of a Tour*, October 7, 1794, p. 92.

A flock of the worst sheep I have seen in the country, were taken into a pen adjoining the road for a man to chuse out a fat one, which he would have some difficulty in accomplishing. He was to have his choice of an ewe for 14/ one of which he expected he could find that would weigh 9 lbs: pr: Q[uarter]: but that seemed doubt-ful. It is a usual practise in buying fat sheep in this country; to agree to pay 1/ pr: lb: for one of the hind quarters, and have all the rest for nothing, which would reduce the carcase to less than /3 p lb:.[63]

The flocks of Rockland probably ran the gamut between these two extremes. They were not specialized. They had not been bred for the quality of their wool. Nor were they intended as meat animals. Instead, they were chosen based on their ability to survive in the harsh Rockland countryside. The sheep were not sheltered or protected from the elements. Constant foraging in the brush and scrub that typified much of Rockland's terrain guaranteed that their fleece was constantly matted and in many cases pulled off in clumps by thorns and other brush. A finely fleeced breed of sheep would be of little value under these conditions.

The sheep roamed at will and were expected to defend them-selves. For this reason horned breeds were preferred. Wolves, pan-thers, and wild cats remained a constant threat to all livestock in Rockland. The mountains that divided old Orange County served as a natural retreat for these predators. The county supervisors attempted to control the wolf population through bounties, but both wolves and cats remained a problem throughout the 18th and into the 19th century. The bounty varied from £2 to £3 a head in the 1780s and 1790s.[64]

Obviously, the predator population remained a problem for farmers in the 1790s and beyond. It would have to be controlled before Rockland's farmers could seriously consider investing in flocks of high-quality sheep. The lack of manpower in Rockland and the rest of New York meant that men were not available to act as shepherds, protecting the flocks. Only the elimination of the wolf and the wild cat from the area could ensure the safety of the flocks.

---

(63)   *Journal of a Tour*, October 9, 1794, p.101.
(64)   "Orange County, N.Y. Board of Supervisors Proceedings, 1723-1798," Budke Collec-tion, BC-9, pp. 249, 284.

Despite the indifferent quality of the wool sheared from local flocks, many of the farm families of Rockland cleaned and spun their own wool, producing wool yarns. Rockland's households kept spinning wheels, both for wool and flax, as well as wool cards and flax hetchels to clean the raw fibers, and reels and swifts to measure the thread and yarn as it was spun. Many households even had their own looms and other weaving paraphernalia.[65] Not all the households wove their own yarn and linen thread into cloth. Some took their yarns to local weavers, men like Tunis Smith, who had learned to weave as a young man. Henry Wansey described a small weaver's establishment that he visited in Woodbridge, New Jersey in 1794. Here he found two men "weaving linen sheeting, out of flax raised and spun by neighbouring families, who brought their yarn to them to make it up into cloth. These men told me they could weave fourteen yards a day of yard-wide sheeting. It was not very fine, as may be supposed."[66]

In all likelihood these weavers, like Tunis Smith, were farmers who wove in the off season or when they had a bit of spare time. Few, if any, of them could survive on weaving alone. It was a valuable skill that could be used to bring in supplemental income. The farm, however, remained the primary source of food and provisions. Weaving brought in a few extras.

Pye's Fulling Mill: Finishing the Wool

Once the wool had been woven into cloth, it still wasn't ready for use. It had to be properly cleaned, dyed, and finished. Fulling mills, like the one operated by David Pye in Clarkstown, performed these services for the local farm families. Although Pye refers to operations at the mill throughout the year, the fall months seem to have been a particularly busy period for his fulling mill.

Fulling is the final cleaning process for woolen yarns and cloth. While the fleece is cleaned by picking out any loose bits of dirt and grass, etc., the wool fibers are greasy. This grease, or lanolin, makes the fibers slightly sticky and easier to spin. This grease has to be

(65)   Looms appear on 7 of the 11 inventories made between 1798 and 1800. See inventories of Bridget Vanderbilt, August, 2, 1798; Harmanus Tallman, August 20, 1798; John Baker, September 24, 1798; Isaac G. Blauvelt, December 3, 1798; Henry J. Eslor, April 22, 1799; Jonah Halstead, January 29, 1800; and Arthur Paul, December 17, 1800, Surrogate's Court, Rockland County.
(66)   *Henry Wansey and His American Journal*, June 24, 1794, p. 125.

removed before the spun yarn, or woven cloth, can be dyed. The grease also must be removed so that the fabric can "bloom," or fibers expand to fill in any air spaces in the weave, producing a soft, warm fabric. David Pye's fulling mill performed these final procedures on his neighbors' homespun fabrics and yarns. In addition to cleaning the homespun fabrics, Pye dyed the yarns and fabrics; tentered, or stretched, the freshly cleaned cloth on square wooden frames so that it dried square; sheared the finished cloth for an even nap; and pressed the cloth.

In his diary David Pye recounted, in laconic terms, how his fulling operations kept him well occupied during the fall of 1785. In October his son John had to repair the dam on the 4th, but the mill was up and running on the 5th when David noted that he was "Pressing and fulling." He continued to use the fulling mill throughout the month, with a slowdown on the 10th as John "mended the mill and began to Collour." On the 11th he "Boiled for Red," "Prest" cloth on the 12th and the 14th, then dyed red again on the 15th, this time with the help of neighbor Jeremiah Fowler. On the 20th John sheared the nap on some of the freshly cleaned cloth but was back to work at fulling on the 21st and made repairs to the rollers. Soap for the fulling process was getting low, so David bought two gallons of soap at a cost of three shillings. Work continued on Saturday, the 22nd, "Fulling & pressing" while David "papered Cloth." The Sabbath was a day of rest for the mill. On this occasion David Pye and his family went to the Clarkstown church to hear Dominie Lansing preach in English. Lansing became ill, however, and did not come. Monday through Wednesday David was back in the mill, dyeing, pressing, and fulling. The extra two gallons of soap purchased on the 21st was running low by the 28th. Daniel Martine came through with the loan of some additional soap. Finally, on the 31st, William Thompson came to work at the mill while David continued "Pressing & Boiling for Red."

November showed a similar mix of pressing, fulling, and dyeing. David finished up his red dye on the 1st, then began a new color on the 11th, "Collourd O. [olive?] Green and L't Coll'r." He tentered the fabric on the 12th, and on the 16th John took up pressing again. John pressed on the 17th, sheared on the 18th, and worked the mill on the 19th. By the 21st "Nothing done in Milln. [sic] Sope [sic] wanting. Making ready to Collour, etc. Pressing." The mill was up and running the next day. John put in a couple of days pressing cloth, then the "Press gave out" on the 26th. The mill was relatively quiet through the end of the month.

On December 2 the press was mended and John was back pressing cloth the next day. Red dye seemed to be popular that fall as David began a new batch on the 8th. (The previous year David did batches of blue and gray on the 6th and brown on the 7th.) The dye pots were still in use on the 13th. John was back at pressing by the 15th. On the 17th the mill was "Fulling Blue" but the soap shortage was critical. Pressing continued, as did the dyeing, but fulling had to await new supplies of soap. On the 21st David got two quarts of soap from A[urt] Polhemus and "sett milln going." It seems obvious that at least for the fall of 1785 David Pye underestimated his need for soap at the mill. His household did not make enough, and it would seem that many of his neighbors lacked a surplus he could buy for use at the mill.

By the end of December, David's concern was to get his books in order, deliver the finished cloth to his neighbors, and collect his fee. Neighbors arrived at the mill both the 26th and the 27th, picking up their finished cloth.

Firewood

One other activity required the ongoing attention of David Pye and all the other residents of Rockland throughout the fall months — the cutting and gathering of wood for the winter months. Survival during Rockland's frigid winters depended on a ready supply of firewood for heat and for cooking. The hills and valleys offered an abundance of readily available wood for home use, but it had to be cut and hauled to the farmhouse, then be allowed to season before it could be used. Throughout the fall, John, David, or one of the slaves returned again and again to the task of cutting and hauling wood to the farm: October 15, "John cutting Wood." October 18, "John about Buckwheat and Cutting Wood." October 19, "John Drawing Wood. Ross Cutting. I paid him for his work." October 21, "Prince cut Wood." October 25, "Joshua Brush cutting up Wood." October 28, "Cutting Wood." November 8, "I drawing fire wood." There is a break in the cutting and drawing of wood through much of November, but then John starts up again on the 23rd when he "went to draw Cordwood." On the 25th John drew "Wood to River."

Obviously wood taken to the Hudson would be of little use in warming a Rockland farmhouse, but it did offer a source of extra cash to Rockland's hard-working farmer. Ever since the Revolutionary War the people of New York City had been desperate for firewood. All the trees on Manhattan had been cut down during the nearly eight years of occupation by the British army. New Jersey, Rockland, and Westchester farmers had a ready-made market for all the firewood they cared to cut and drag out of the forests. As early as 1784 travelers in the area remarked on the stacks of firewood that stood on the docks in Rockland, waiting for market sloops to carry them to the city. The sloops made as many trips as they could during the fall, as New York City householders stockpiled wood against the upcoming cold. Once the Hudson froze, wood stood in stacks at the docks, waiting for the thaw that would allow traffic between New York City and the hinterland to resume. Rockland's farmers were active participants in this trade, a fact readily apparent to Francisco de Miranda in 1784:

> Three miles farther on we found the small town of Haverstraw, situated exactly on the bank of the North River, where we noticed an enormous quantity of firewood; this was to be sent to New York whenever the ice should desist and permit the navigation of the river, because so great a shortage was being experienced there that a cartload of firewood was worth twenty or thirty pesos.[67]

An industrious farmer in Rockland at least did not have to worry about a lack of firewood to keep him and his family warm throughout the winter. The rugged, mountainous terrain that characterized Rockland pretty much guaranteed that trees would be available in abundance. Such an abundance provided at least one thing Rockland's residents could be thankful for as the new year approached and the old year ended.

David Pye and his neighbors remembered this and other blessings as they gathered in church on December 25 to celebrate Christmas. Christmas was a religious holiday in the 1790s, with few if any secular trappings. Rockland's farm families attended a church service, then went home. They returned to church for another sermon on the 26th,

---

(67) *Travels of Francisco de Miranda in the United States, 1783-1784*, ca. February 23, 1784, p. 92.

Boxing Day in the English tradition. Unlike Christmas, which was frequently spent in solitude, the 26th was a day set aside to entertain friends, neighbors, and family who came to call. David Pye and his family had "Company all day" in 1785. It was in many ways a time to wrap up the events of the old year and take stock so that you were prepared for whatever might be needed in the new.

Winter:
January, February, and March

> In our climate..., the farmers are necessarily hurried with their business during much the greater part of the year, that is, from April to November inclusive. But in the winter, they may be in some danger of spending some of their time idly, if they do not take some care to prevent it. Feeding and tending their cattle, if they do it faithfully, will take some considerable part of each day, if the stock be large. The dressing of hemp and flax requires some time, and ought to be done in winter. Getting home fewel [fuel] for maintaining fires through the year, and hauling stuff and fitting it for the building and repair of fences; threshing and cleaning of corn and grain, and preparing farming implements, may all be done at this season. And these things ought to be done at this time of year, to prevent hurry at a more busy season. So that, though our farmers cannot plough, or do any thing to the soil in winter, unless it be sometimes in part of December, they need not be idle.[68]

If spring, summer, and fall were characterized by a sense of urgency — the need to get one more thing done before it rained, or while the sun shone, or before the harvest — winter was characterized by a sense of leisure. With the ground frozen and under a layer of ice and snow, field work had to stop. This was the period when tools could be mended or new tools made. Activities that might have been postponed during the rush of fall chores could be resumed, activities such

---

(68)   Deane, *Georgical Dictionary*, p. 98.

as spinning or weaving. Men and women who had special skills now had the opportunity to use them.

John Wallace of Clarkstown, for example, had some skill with a needle. Perhaps he had apprenticed with a tailor at some point in his life. He traveled around Rockland during the winter months, making clothes for the farmers. He showed up at David Pye's on January 27, 1785 and stayed to make a coat for John Pye. Over in Westchester Mrs. Lee stayed at Silas Constant's in January 1796, making breeches for the Reverend Mr. Constant. In February 1790, Josiah Ingersoll stopped at the clergyman's house to make a coat while Mr. Golden stopped by and made up some shoes for the Constant household.[69] In all these cases, the tailoring and shoemaking probably supplemented the income these itinerants earned either on their own farms or as laborers during the summer on someone else's farm. The winter snows freed up enough time for people like John Wallace and Josiah Ingersoll to practice their other trade, earning a little extra money for themselves and providing specialized services for the larger Rockland community.

David Pye continued many of the activities that had filled up the fall months — running the fulling mill as long as the creek was not frozen and pressing and cutting cloth as time and other work permitted. The slower winter months provided the perfect opportunity to catch up on bookkeeping and to settle accounts as he traveled around the county on various business matters. He appears to have had a reputation as a man who was handy with mechanical things, for many of his neighbors brought their watches to him to be repaired. Thus, on January 20, 1785, after carrying out a variety of errands, Pye put a chain "on [a] lawyer's watch and cleaned Denines watch." Two days later he spent "Most part of the day about Watches and other odd things." At the end of the month, January 29, he fixed D. Coe's watch and E. Smith's. Then, when visiting Philip Sarvent of Nyack on February 14, Pye "Cleaned his Clock and rec'd pay for my work."

Winter Hauling

For Pye and other Rockland residents, hauling heavy loads from the woods and fields carried over from the late fall into the winter months. In fact, winter was an even better time to haul materials around

---

(69) Roebling, *Journal of the Rev. Silas Constant*, January 15, 1796; February 2 & 15, 1790.

the county. Again and again, Pye and some of his men spent the day gathering hay or chopping wood in the woods and sledding it back. "John fetched 5 load[s] wood, 2 mine, 3 Andrew Onderdonk's." "Went this morning to get some people to fetch my hay from the pond...." "Went for the hay, had seven sleds besides my own. Brought home all the stack and returned by ½ past one o'clock." "Went this morning to draw wood out of swamp at Doctor's."[70] The wood was either intended for the household fireplace or stove for heat, or it could have been stockpiled for future shipment downriver to New York.

Fields and roadways covered in snow made it possible to haul these loads of wood, stone, or hay with relative ease during the winter months. This was the best season for hauling. Sleds moved easily over the snow, making winter the one season of the year when heavy loads were unlikely to be bogged down in mud. Wagons and carts that might break an axle or a wheel on the heavily rutted roads of summer and fall, glided easily over the frozen surface on wooden runners. Tunis Smith and his father began cutting the timber they would need to build their saw mill in January 1795. They sledded the timber from the woods to the site of their new saw mill during the winter months. They had the lumber cut and ready for the carpenter, who arrived at the mill site in April and raised the frame for the mill.[71]

The snow that facilitated the swift movement of heavy loads also accommodated the most enjoyable activities of the winter months, sledding and visiting. While farmers seldom had time during the rest of the year simply to visit friends and relatives, the winter months saw a steady stream of visitors.

New Year's Celebrations

The visiting began with New Year's celebrations. "Company to keep New Year. Sermon at Church....Young people drinking wine. Broke glasses." With these words, David Pye described his New Year's celebration of 1785. His New Year appears to have been relatively quiet, but it had all the elements of a traditional New Year in 18th-century New York: company, a church service, drink, and possibly a little rowdiness that ended with a few broken glasses. Other accounts of late

---

(70) *David Pye Diary*, January 5, 15, 17, & 18, 1785.
(71) Tunis Smith, "Remembrance," p. 52.

18th-century New Year's festivities depict the same qualities but with a little more noise and exuberance:

> I had traveled far enough during the day to hope for a quiet sleep, and expected a good night; but at four in the morning I was awakened by a musket fired close to my windows: I listened but heard not the smallest noise or motion in the street, which made me imagine it was some musket which had gone off by itself without causing any accident. So I attempted to go back to sleep. A quarter of an hour later a fresh musket or pistol shot interrupted my repose: this was followed by several others; so that I no longer had any doubt that it was some rejoicing or feast, like our village christenings. The hour indeed struck me as unusual, but at length a number of voices mingled with musketry, shouting "New Year," reminded me that it was the first of January, and I concluded that it was thus that *Messieurs les Américains* celebrated the beginning of the new year. Though this manner of proclaiming it was not, I must own, especially pleasing to me, there was nothing to do but be patient; but at the end of half an hour I heard a confused noise of upwards of a hundred persons, mostly children or young people, assembled under my windows. Soon I was even better warned of their proximity, for they fired several musket shots, knocked rudely at the door, and threw stones against my windows. Cold and indolence still kept me in bed, but M. Lynch got up, and came into my chamber to tell me that these people certainly meant to do me honor and to ask me for some money. I requested him to go down and give them two louis; he found them already masters of the house and drinking my landlord's rum. In a quarter of an hour they went off to visit other streets and continued their noise until daylight.[72]

---

(72)   Marquis de Chastellux, *Travels in North America in the Years 1780, 1781, and 1782*, rev. trans. with introd. and notes by Howard C. Rice, Jr., 2 vols. (Chapel Hill, N.C.: Published for the Institute of Early American History and Culture by The University of North Carolina Press, 1963), 1:222-223.

Visiting, during the day rather than the middle of the night as experienced above by the Marquis de Chastellux in 1780-1781, made up a significant portion of the New Year's celebration. David Pye's company would have been greeted with plenty of food and drink. The New Year offered the opportunity for conviviality, good wishes for the next year, and commiseration or congratulations on the year gone by. Families of both English and Dutch ancestry brought in the New Year in this fashion with each group adding a slightly different element to the holiday. Nineteenth-century commentators on the customs of "olden times" thanked the Dutch for the various special treats offered to visitors: "*Oly Cookes, Pretzies, Kiskatomas-nuts* and *Spitzenburgs,* with hot spiced *Santa Cruz, good strong Christmas beer* and *cider.*"[73] Gift giving on New Year's was associated with the English and the French rather than the Dutch, although it is not clear how prevalent this custom became. Certainly New York City newspapers displayed advertisements for New Year's gifts beginning at the turn of the century.[74] Regardless of whether gifts were exchanged, for both the English and the Dutch this was the secular holiday of the winter. Christmas in the 18th century remained a religious commemoration. New Year's was a time to let loose.

> The New Year's day with us, almost from time immemorial, was ushered in with great noise and rejoicing, which was formerly continued throughout the day and even the day following. The inhabitants used to go from house to house with their guns and fire salutes; and at every house thus saluted, it was customary to invite them in to partake of the good things of the season. After enjoying themselves for a time, in eating and drinking, they would depart accompanied by the men of the house, and thus they would pass through the whole neighborhood, until every house was saluted, and all the men of the vicinity were collected together — then they would

---

(73) Gabriel Furman, *Antiquities of Long Island*, to which is added a bibliography by Henry Onderdonk, Jr., ed. Frank Moore (New York: J.W. Bouton, 1875), pp. 261-262.
(74) *Arts & Crafts in New York, 1800-1804*, Rita Susswein Gottesman, comp., Collections of The New-York Historical Society for the Year 1949 (New York: The New-York Historical Society, 1965), January 1, 1802, p. 389.

go to some convenient spot and pass the remainder of
the day in firing at the mark and in athletic sports.[75]

Sled, Sleighs, and Skates

It was the sled that allowed all this visitation between neighbors
and family, just as it was the sled that enabled the farmers of Rockland
to haul wood and stones from distant wood lots and fields. The work
sled, or sledge, was essentially a flatbed placed on wooden runners.
Because it was low to the ground, farmers could load wood or heavy
stone relatively easily, minimizing the height heavy objects had to be
lifted. Posts could be attached to the side to prevent loads from slipping
sidewise.

Pleasure sleds, or sleighs, had low sides, bench seats, and a high
back, but like the work sled they rode low to the ground on a flatbed.
Mme. de la Tour du Pin, spending her first winter in the Mohawk
Valley, described her sleigh, one typical of these late 18th-century
pleasure vehicles:

> We already owned four good horses and two work
> sledges. A third was kept for our personal use and was
> known as the "pleasure sledge." It held six people and
> was rather like a very shallow box. At the back was the
> main bench, a little wider than the remainder of the
> sledge, it was mounted over a cupboard which served to
> hold small packages. It had a back-piece higher than
> head level so that it sheltered us from the wind. The
> other benches, two in number, were just ordinary planks.
> Buffalo skins and sheepskins kept our feet warm. Two
> horses drew this sledge and it could travel very fast.[76]463

The sleighs sped swiftly and quietly over the frozen fields and
roads, so quietly that sleigh bells were a necessity. They served to warn
unwary pedestrians of a fast-approaching sleigh, especially at night.
Edward Dixon, spending his first winter in Westchester, much enjoyed
the "music" of the sleigh:

---

(75) Furman, *Antiquities of Long Island*, pp. 258-259.
(76) *Memoirs of Madame de la Tour du Pin*, pp. 250-251.

They will go upon the snow, (which is some winters 3 feet and more deep) with slays (or as we call them Sleds) neatly adapted for the same use. There is generally little wind here, which makes the snow fall level, then the heat of the sun at noon soon makes it bear Horses, slays or any thing. On the Post road in snow the slays go jingling past, fifteen in a day, with some ten bells at their pair of Horses, very pleasant to hear. It is against the Law to go without Bells at slays only for which a man maybe [fined?], many having been struck at night time. They go amazing swift & might come upon one unperceived if without their music.[77]

Sleighs made river crossings potentially much easier and faster, but also potentially much more dangerous. Once the Hudson River was frozen, ferries could no longer be used and local residents had to trust to the thickness of the ice to allow them to cross between Rockland and Westchester. Francisco de Miranda, traveling through the valley in the winter of 1783-1784, crossed and recrossed the river between Verplanck's Point and West Point in February 1784. He and his party left Peekskill on February 21, heading across the river on a sleigh:

The next day we continued our journey over the ice of the North River, the surface of which had the appearance of a very polished and handsome lamina. The ice must have been two feet thick, and the snow on top of this one and a half feet; we did not have the least misgiving about danger, for, although it has broken many times in those places where the wind introduces itself between the surface of the water and the mass of ice, the way was already so beaten with the multitude of sledges which came and went on the river that there was no basis for the least care.[78]

They were bound upriver to visit West Point, the scene of Benedict Arnold's treachery during the American Revolution.

---

(77)   Edward Dixon to George Dixon, December 23, 1800, Ossining Historical Society, Ossining, N.Y.
(78)   *Travels of Francisco de Miranda*, pp. 83-84.

De Miranda and his party spent a day in the West Point area, then headed downriver. The first leg of their journey took them from West Point to Verplanck's Point. They accommodated themselves "very well in two sledges and went down the river over the ice, like lightning....Continuing our Laplandish route over the ice, we arrived at Verplancks Point, seven miles farther down, where we went on land." After a short visit on land, they returned to the river, this time heading across toward Stony Point, but with considerably less confidence in the solidity of the ice:

> From Kings Ferry we crossed the river over the ice, with no slight misgiving, for in some places the water penetrated and the ice was known to be quite thin, but comforting us were a good guide we had in front and a stick in the hand to support ourselves should our feet open a large hole. So we all crossed on foot, sending before the sledge and horses for greater safety.[79]

Not all sleds were horse drawn, and not all runners were on sleds. The hills of Rockland meant sledding for the children; the ponds and streams meant skating. Both of these recreations followed the Dutch and Northern European settlers from Europe to North America, and the people of Rockland undoubtedly enjoyed these traditional winter amusements, just like their counterparts in other parts of the Hudson Valley. When reminiscing about winters in Albany in the 1760s, Anne Grant recalled the small sleds that filled Albany's main street, a great sledding hill, and her own rather timid excursion into the world of sledding:

> Every boy and youth in town, from eight to eighteen, had a little low sledge, made with a rope like a bridle to the front, by which it could be dragged after one by the hand. On this one or two at most could fit, and this sloping descent being made as smooth as a looking glass, by sliders' sledges, &c. perhaps a hundred at once set out in succession from the top of this street, each seated in his little sledge with the rope in his hand, which, drawn to the right or left, served to guide him. He

---

(79) *Travels of Francisco de Miranda,* p. 90.

pushed it off with a little stick, as one would launch a boat; and then, with the most astonishing velocity, precipitated by the weight of the owner, the little machine glided past, and was at the lower end of the street in an instant. What could be so peculiarly delightful in this rapid and smooth descent, I could never discover; though in a more retired place, and on a smaller scale, I have tried the amusement; but to a young Albanian, slaying, as he called it, was one of the first joys of life, though attended with the drawback of walking to the top of the declivity dragging his sledge every time he renewed his flight, for such it might well be called. In the managing of this little machine some dexterity was necessary; an unskillful Phaeton was sure to fall. The conveyance was so low, that a fall was attended with little danger, yet with much disgrace, for an universal laugh from all sides assailed the fallen charioteer.[80]

While sledding appealed to the youths, skating appears to have been practiced by all ages. Alexander Coventry, up in Hudson, New York, bought himself a pair of skates for eight shillings. He bought them on January 10, then tried them out for the first time on the 14th. He skated on the Hudson, sharing the ice with several sleighs that spent the afternoon "passing and repassing" over the icy surface.[81] His skating was for recreation, pure and simple. Others found skating a good alternative to walking if you lacked a horse. Philip Van Cortlandt, of Croton, recalled skating down the Hudson from Peekskill to Croton during the winter of 1777. He wanted to check on the family manor house, to see how much damage had been incurred to date as a result of the Revolution. He then skated back up the river, returning to his regiment.

Anne Grant, again recalling her experiences in the Albany area in the third quarter of the 18th century, probably best summarized the unique winter experience for all New Yorkers:

> In winter, the river, frozen to a great depth, formed the principal road through the country, and was the scene of

(80)   *Memoirs of an American Lady*, pp. 105-106.
(81)   "Memoirs of an Emigrant," p. 86.

all those amusements of skating and sledge races, common to the north of Europe. They used in great parties to visit their friends at a distance, and having an excellent and hardy breed of horses, flew from place to place over the snow or ice in these sledges with incredible rapidity, stopping a little while at every house they came to, and always well received, whether acquainted with the owners or not. The night never impeded these travellers, for the atmosphere was so pure and serene, and the snow so reflected the moon and star-light, that the nights exceeded the days in beauty.[82]

Rocklanders, like their counterparts throughout the state, participated fully in the joys and frivolities of the winter months. This was the period to refresh one's body and mind, to visit with friends, to simply enjoy traveling smoothly and quickly between distant farms. It was a welcome respite from the continuous labor needed about the farm during the spring, summer, and fall. Samuel Deane exhorted his readers not to overindulge in the spirit of leisure during the winter months, but to prepare for the upcoming spring. Undoubtedly Rockland's residents used the slow period for both purposes, relaxation and preparation.

Chapter 4

The People of Rockland County in the 1790s

As David Pye looked out over the crowd assembled at Harmanus (Harmoney) Tallman's farm, he remembered a cold winter's day 13 years earlier. Rebecca had sent word that her husband was ill, failing fast. He wanted to prepare his will. David and Cathrena had gone down to Nyack that Sunday, the 13th of February, and spent the night. David and Harmoney spent quite a while going over the will. Then Harmoney signed it the next day. Harmoney knew he was dying, but at least he could be assured he had taken care of his family. Now everything was God's will. Abraham, Harmoney's son, had stopped by a couple of days later to say that his father had worsened. In a week Tallman was dead. David and Cathrena had attended his funeral on a cold Monday. Now, with Rebecca's death, Harmanus Tallman's final wishes could be carried out.[1]

The crowd at the Tallman house murmured in approval as the vendue master, or auctioneer, brought out the last remaining auction lots. Rebecca and Harmanus's sons, Abraham and Tunis, and their grandson, Jacob De Clark, had been among the more active bidders. The

(1) According to Harmanus Tallman's will, drawn February 14, 1785 and filed August 16, 1798, his wife had full use of his estate until her death or remarriage. At that time, the estate was to be sold and divided equally among his three sons, Tunis, Harmanus, and Abraham, and his daughter Naltie, wife of Jacobus De Clark. Budke Collection, B-35.

Articles of the Vendue of the Goods and Chattles of Rebecka Tallman Deceased holden the 3 day of September 1790.

1st The Highest bidder shall be deemed the buyer and if any difference arise between two bidders the goods to be put up to Sale again.

2d All persons buying any goods and chattles at this Vendue may have time to make payment until the first day of March next and if not then paid to become lawfull Intrest from the said first day of March until paid Except that any person buying less then the sum of Ten Shillings at this Vendue the Monies in that case to be immediatly paid.

3d Any Goods bought at this Vendue that cannot be now taken away such as Corn Buckwheat &c a Sufficient time shall be given to take away the same as well as the Grain Hay and Flax in the Barn.

4th Any person buying any goods at this Vendue to give immediate Security for the payment of the Monies when they shall become due if required and on such refusal the said Goods to be sold again at the Expen. of the first buyer.

           James H Tallmon
           Abraham H Tallman
           Executors

N.B. the monies arrising in this Vendue to be paid to James H Tallman and Abraham H Tallman Executors

The articles for the vendue of the "Rebecka" Tallman estate set out the basic procedures for bidding on items at the estate auction and the terms for payment at the auction. "Articles of the Vendue of the Goods and Chattles of Rebecka Tallman Deceased," September 3, 1798.

Budke Collection, BC-79,
Rare Books and Manuscripts Division, The New York Public Library.

vendue, however, was a major event for the local Orangetown (Nyack) and southern Clarkstown communities.[2]

More than 40 bidders from Orangetown and Clarkstown, with their families, gathered at the old Tallman house September 15, 1798. The vendue provided an opportunity for friends and neighbors to meet and socialize while they looked over the possessions of the Tallmans and decided what to add to their own homes and farms. While any auction could draw a good crowd, the sale of all the personal possessions of prominent citizens such as grist mill owner Harmanus Tallman and his wife Rebecca Snedeker Tallman guaranteed that the entire neighborhood would be present.

While the men bid on individual items, paying attention to the advice of their wives about needed household goods, the women ensured that there was plenty of food and shared the latest news of family and friends. The children, usually restricted to their sisters and brothers and near neighbors for playmates, enjoyed this unusual opportunity to renew acquaintances and play with more distant kin and neighbors.

At this vendue, the children and grandchildren of Rebecca and Harmanus Tallman successfully bid on many of the items from the estate. Tunis bought his father's silver watch for £5.7.0. Abraham bought several of his mother's quilts and coverlets (£5.13.0). Jacob De Clark, Rebecca and Harmanus's grandson, did particularly well. Having started his own household within the last few years, Jacobus still needed a variety of tools for his farm as well as furnishings for his home. That September he added a fireplace trammel, two bed ticks, shovel and tongs, an oval table, clothes chest, corner cupboard, warming pan, silver tablespoon, and small wheel to his household furnishings. He also bought three scythes, a

---

(2)   "Articles of the Vendue of the Goods and Chattles of Rebecka Tallman Deceased holden the 3rd Day of September 1798." Tunis H. Tallman, Abraham H. Tallman, Exec. Budke Collection, BC-79. "An Inventory of the Goods and Chattles of Harmanus Tallman Deceased of Orangetown in the County of Rockland taken the 20th day of August 1798 by Order and under the Direction of Thunis & Abraham Tallman, Surviving Executors," Surrogate's Court, Rockland County. The inventory of Harmanus Tallman is identical to the vendue list of the estate of Rebecca Tallman, taken September 15, 1798. Budke Collection, BC-79.

windmill, a hatchel, and some salt for the farm. All this, for only £11.16.4.

Other neighbors, from both Clarkstown and Nyack, bid on the tools and produce of the farm. The livestock, horses, cattle, and hogs were particularly valuable. David Pye, Jr., of Clarkstown, added a black mare (£12.10.0) and a hog (£2.4.0) to his farm stock. Lambert Smith of Clarkstown bought a white-backed cow for £8.0.0. John S. Smith got a deal on two hogs for £1.11.0. Altogether the Tallman's five cattle (including a young bull), eleven hogs, four horses, and a dog brought in £84.2.8. The crops in the field and in the barn and barracks brought the estate an additional £36.19.0.

By the end of the vendue, the Tallman heirs had £162.16.2 to divide equally among themselves. Valuable manufactured goods, textiles, furniture, pots, pans, farm equipment, and livestock had been redistributed among the neighbors, ensuring their continued use. The successful bidders could be happy with their new possessions. Others simply enjoyed the opportunity to meet their neighbors in a congenial environment, exchanging information, gossip, or family news, depending on the inclination of the participants. Most of all, the vendue was a distinct change of pace from the day-in, day-out routine that characterized rural, agricultural Rockland County in the 1790s.

The Will of a Dutch Farmer

The vendue of Rebecca and Harmanus Tallman's estate in Nyack in the fall of 1798 provides a great deal of insight into the lives of the residents of Rockland County at the end of the 18th century. Even as they approached the opening of a new century, the Tallmans and their neighbors in Orangetown and Clarkstown along the Hudson River remained firmly tied to the traditions and lifestyles of their rural, primarily Dutch ancestors.

When Harmanus Tallman died in February 1785, he left "full use" of his estate to his wife until her death or until she remarried. On her death or remarriage, the estate was to be divided among their children. Harmanus had given Rebecca temporary control over his property for the duration of her widowhood alone, rather than complete control over the disposition of their property. This did not mean that he did not trust her to see that their children inherited his property upon her death. Rather, it reflected the legal limitations placed on women in 18th- and 19th-century New York.

If Rebecca married a second time, all her property — including anything left outright to her in Harmanus Tallman's will — would come under the legal control of her second husband. She would lose the ability to dispose of it as she saw fit. Only widows retained complete control over their own property and arranged for its disposition. The only way Harmanus could guarantee that his children would eventually inherit the estate was to give Rebecca control for life but stipulate its eventual distribution among their sons and daughter.[3]

The will also provided for the equal distribution of the property among the Tallmans' sons and one daughter. This followed the Dutch tradition of equal shares among all children, both sons and daughters. English tradition favored the eldest son as recipient of the principal inheritance (primogeniture), while any other children received significantly reduced shares. The will paid lip service to the eldest son's special position in the family when it set aside £1.5.0 for Tunis as his "birthright" as the eldest. Ultimately, all the heirs benefited equally.

Although Harmanus provided for the equal distribution of his estate among the heirs, some special bequests had to be made. The recognition of Tunis's birthright as eldest son was one such bequest. The disposition of Harmanus Tallman's two "Negro boys," Will and Tom, represented another specific inheritance. Harmanus (Jr.) and Tunis received equal shares in Will while Abraham got Tom. African slaves, like Tom and Will, formed an integral part of the Rockland community in the 18th century, especially in the riverside townships of Orangetown and Clarkstown. Africans, both enslaved and free, accounted for 8% of the Rockland population in 1790 and nearly 10% in

---

(3)   Similar provisions for the wife to inherit for the remainder of her life or until she remarried can be found in many other wills of the period. See also Will of Jonah Halstead, Hempstead, drawn April 3, 1790, Budke Collection, BC-73; Will of Uldrich Brower, Clarkstown, drawn April 17, 1793, BC-78.

The estate inventory for Harmanus Tallman illustrates the wide variety of furnishings and manufactured goods available to well-to-do Rockland County families at the end of the 18th century.

Estate inventory, Harmanus Tallman, August 20, 1798,
Rockland County Surrogate's Court, New City, New York.
Photo by Jeffrey Hunter.

1800.[4] Harmanus may have arranged it so that his slaves would not be sold at auction, like the rest of his property, but both law and custom regarded them as personal property, not as people.

The Tallman Estate Auction

While Harmanus Tallman's will illustrates the legal framework in which property rights were maintained in 1790s Rockland, the 1798 sale of the Tallman estate provides additional insights into social and economic conditions in Rockland at the end of the 18th century. The vendue list identifies the successful bidders. From the list we can determine that the attendees came from the immediate neighborhood of Nyack and southern Clarkstown.[5] Transportation difficulties in the county limited the attendance to the immediate neighborhood, despite the interest generated by such a sale.

Like the Tallmans, the majority of those who attended the vendue were of Dutch ancestry, reflecting the strong concentration of Dutch settlers in the older, settled areas along the Hudson River, such as Tappan and Nyack. Also like the Tallmans, many of the bidders came from Rockland's wealthier households. More than one-third of them had been appraised by the local tax assessor as having property valued in excess of £100. Fifteen of the successful bidders owned slaves. Other participants were young farmers of limited means, just setting up their households and farms.[6]

---

(4)   *First Census.* "Federal Census 1800." In the 1790 census, the residents of the future Rockland County are enumerated under Orange County in the towns of Orangetown and Haverstraw. By 1800 Rockland County existed as a separate unit with four towns: Orangetown, Clarkstown, New Hempstead, and Haverstraw.

(5)   See Survey for the Nyack Turnpike, 1817, by Tunis Smith, for households around Tallman's mill. Collections of The Historical Society of Rockland County, A88.10.2. The majority of these near neighbors attended the sale.

(6)   "Clarkstown District Tax List for 1787, Major John Smith, Collector," Budke Collection, BC-52; "Tax List for Orangetown, N.Y. for the Year 1796, Abraham G. Blauvelt, Collector," Budke Collection, BC-23. Slave ownership is established through the 1790 and 1800 federal census reports.

The vendue list records not only who acquired the various items offered at the auction, it also identifies what they bought and how much they paid. The assortment of personal and household goods available to late 18th-century Rockland County residents, as well as their relative worth, is evident. Most of the items are utilitarian: pots, pans, trammels for the fireplaces, dishes, tubs, and barrels. Others, such as the cupboard purchased by Peter Oblenis for £5.3.0, or the square looking glass bought for £1.6.0, indicate the premium value placed on fine furnishings. Textiles, particularly bed hangings, curtains, quilts, and coverlets were also highly sought after. John Conklin of Orangetown bid £2.4.6 for a set of curtains, probably intended for a bedstead. A feather bed, bolster, and pillow set went for £6, making a complete bed set, minus bed tick, worth over £8, the single most expensive piece of furniture in the house.

It was the farm implements, the crops, and the livestock, however, that accounted for most of the interest in the auction. They were by far the most valuable portion of the estate. Nearly three-quarters of the £162.16.2 brought in by the auction came from the sale of the Tallman livestock and crops. Livestock alone — horses, cattle, and hogs — accounted for more than £84 in sales. Crops that Rebecca had put in that year — wheat, rye, buckwheat, turnips, potatoes, broom corn, and hay — brought in an additional £37.

The high value placed on farm-related items underscored the critical role played by farming in Rockland. Farming was the most important industry in Rockland in the 1790s, just as it had been throughout the 18th century. Other industries in Rockland also processed the bounty of the land in one form or another. The grist mills ground grain, the fulling mills cleaned freshly woven textiles, and the saw mills split and sawed lumber. Industries based on the extraction of mineral wealth, such as the iron industry in Rockland, Orange, Passaic, and Bergen counties and the newly opened Pierson nail manufactory in Ramapo, also processed the wealth of the land. However, agriculture remained premier, and the value placed on the agricultural tools, equipment, and livestock at the Tallman farm mirrored this basic fact of life in the 1790s.

Literacy and Education

The will, inventory, and auction for Harmanus and Rebecca Tallman's estate also make it clear that education in Rockland was quite rudimentary, especially by modern standards. Spelling was idiosyncratic, to say the least. It was loosely phonetic, based on how the writer pronounced the words. Thus an Englishman spelled one way, a Dutchman spelled another. Similarly, an Englishman might record the will of Herman Tallman while a Dutchman recorded the inventory of Harmanus Tallman.

The inventory and vendue list reveal these kinds of differences in spelling and identification of individuals. They also make it clear that Abraham H. and Tunis H. Tallman, executors of the estate and prominent residents of Orangetown, could hardly write their names. David Pye drew up the estate inventory and oversaw the vendue list, both of which are quite legible. As executors, Abraham and Tunis signed each document. Their signatures are barely legible. Obviously, neither Abraham nor Tunis was comfortable writing, a common situation even among the wealthiest members of Rockland society.[7]

The general low level of education reflected a lack of opportunity rather than a lack of interest in education. Throughout the 18th century, education was the responsibility of the parents, not of the broader community. There was no formal system of education. If there was sufficient interest in a community for the parents to hire a schoolmaster, a small school would be established. In areas with widely scattered farms, there weren't the resources needed to employ a teacher. Here parents, if able, taught their children the rudiments of reading and writing.

By the end of the 18th century, the state government had begun to take an interest in the education of its citizens. In 1795 the state legislature passed "An Act for the encouragement of schools." For the first time New York State specifically allocated state revenues for the use of local schools. It also required that the individual towns raise a

---

(7)   Of the bidders at the vendue, Tunis H. Tallman ranked second in wealth and Abraham H. Tallman ranked fourth, based on the 1796 Orangetown tax assessments. Tunis was assessed a total £628; Abraham's property was valued at £455. Only Peter De Pew, also of Orangetown, had a higher appraisal, with his property valued at £818 in 1796. "Tax List for Orangetown, 1796."

sum equal to one-half the state appropriation for schools in each town. The combined state and local funds would be used to support local schools.[8]

The law allowed freeholders in each town to elect from three to seven persons to act as commissioners of schools. These commissioners sent annual accounts of the schools within their district to the office of the Secretary of State. The annual return included the name of the schoolmaster, the dates of instruction, the names of students who attended each school, and the total number of days each student attended. The moneys raised under the act would be distributed in each township according to the total number of days for which instruction was provided in each of the schools.

The returns for the township of Clarkstown at the end of the 18th century have survived. They make it clear that the number of students in each school and the number of days each student attended class varied dramatically. There was a total of 10 schools in Clarkstown at the end of the century. In addition, some children who lived in Clarkstown attended schools in Hempstead, undoubtedly because they were closer.[9]

Attendance was strictly voluntary. Parents and guardians sent their children to school or kept them at home, as they saw fit. The schools operated on a quarterly basis and depending on local demand, could be open all year round. For example, Andrew Tinkey, schoolmaster at the Stone School House at Taulman's Corners from April 4, 1796 to February 28, 1797, taught a total of 56 students over the 11 months he held classes. Six of his pupils — Isaac Vanderbilt (son of Johannes), Harvey and Jenny Brewer, Mary and Jacob Blauvelt, and Isaac Vanderbilt (son of Derick) — each attended 219 days. John Van Orden, on the other hand, attended only 12 days. The average number of days attended was 153. Abraham DeBaun, schoolmaster at the Nanuet Meadow School, taught just 18 students between April 18, 1796 and March 1797. Peter Demarest attended school a total of 217 days,

(8) See introd., *Returns of the Schools of the Town of Clarkstown for the Years 1796, 1797, 1798, and 1799*, introd. and notes by George H. Budke, Budke Collection, BC-51, The New York Public Library, Manuscripts & Archives Division (Library Association of Rockland County, 1975). [Hereafter referred to as *Returns of the Clarkstown Schools.*]

(9)   The 10 schools were Street, New City, Sandhill, Clarkstown, Caspersberg, Nyack, Pond next to the house of Christian DeBaun, Nanuet Meadow, Unity Hall, and Stone School House. In addition, Clarkstown students attended the New Hempstead School and the school at the English Meeting House in Hempstead. See *Returns of the Clarkstown Schools.*

and Jacob Elison came only 51 days. On average, DeBaun's students received 140 days of instruction during the year.

Similarly, the Street School was open nearly year-round, although the trustees changed schoolmasters in November 1796. Thomas Howard, Jr., taught 50 students April-November 1796. During this period Jacob Secor attended school 150 days while Daniel Cocolect came only 23 days. The average student attended 71 days. During the winter months school attendance dropped dramatically. Isaac B. Van Houten was now schoolmaster, but he had only 18 pupils between December 1796 and March 1797. Jacob Secor once again attended most diligently, with 57 days of instruction. William Slott attended only eight times. Students at Street School averaged 44 days of school during the winter months.

Both boys and girls went to school, although the Clarkstown records indicate that boys outnumbered girls at most of the schools. Slightly over one-third of all the students attending Clarkstown schools in 1796-1797 were females. There is no way to establish the ages of the students, but they undoubtedly ranged from five to seven years old at one end up to teenagers at the other end.

The school curriculum was basic — reading, writing, and arithmetic. The goal was to produce a literate population that could read when necessary, write, and undertake basic arithmetic computations when needed. Surviving exercise books from the turn of the century show arithmetic problems focusing on everyday activities, such as converting dollars and cents into pounds, shillings, and pence or determining basic measurements, such as yardage for cloth. A successful student should be able to carry out the normal business of life without problems. He should also be sufficiently literate as to understand important political concerns and vote with intelligent forethought at the local and national elections.

Currency

The inventory and vendue lists also illustrate another aspect of life that was changing for Rockland's residents as the century ended. New Yorkers had long used a variety of currencies but generally based their monetary transactions on the British system of pounds, shillings, and pence. This continued to be true in New York and the United States as a whole until the end of the 18th century. As of July 1, 1797, however, all official records and transactions in New York changed to the decimal-based dollar and cents, with one dollar valued at four-tenths of a New York pound (£1 equals \$2.50).[10] The inventory of Harmanus Tallman's estate, filed as an official document with the Surrogate's Court in New City, valued the estate in the newly mandated dollars and cents. The vendue record, which was not intended for official filing, gave all valuations in terms of pounds, shillings, and pence. For several years, well into the early 19th century, residents of Rockland and throughout the United States used both systems of currency, with the older, English-based system gradually disappearing.

Tradition and Diversity

The continuance of the old with the occasional introduction of something new, these were the characteristics of life in Rockland County in the 1790s. Old customs and traditions based on life in an agricultural community remained strong. Residents of English and Dutch ancestry remained faithful to their own language and religion, in some instances perpetuating national prejudices. All needed to speak and understand English, the official language of the country, but many were more comfortable in Dutch, the language spoken in their homes.

This mixture of English and Dutch, the old and the young, Africans, whites, and Native Americans was not uniform throughout Rockland. Instead, different townships exhibited quite different population characteristics. Orangetown's inhabitants were older, more mature, with fewer children, more Dutchmen, and greater wealth.

---

(10)   "An Act relative to the money of account of this State," January 27, 1797, Chap. 9, 20th Sess., *Laws of the State of New York*, 4:9.

Haverstraw's residents, on the other hand, were younger, a more diverse mixture of English and Dutch, and significantly poorer. The people in Clarkstown and Hempstead fell somewhere in between. An examination of some of these diversities, as they existed in 1790 and 1800, brings some of the unique characteristics of Rockland at the end of the 18th century into sharp focus.

Rocklanders in the 1790 and 1800 Census

Susanna Burray had become a problem. She was a widow, elderly, unable to support herself. Too infirm to work, she had "become Chargeable to the Towns of Haverstraw, Clarks Town & New Hemstead." In other words, she was too poor to provide for herself, and the local overseers of the poor had to pay for her food, clothing, lodging, and any other expenses. Although the town fathers readily acknowledged the town's responsibility to provide for its own poor, Susanna seemed a special case. After all, she might be poor and her husband dead, but she had five grandsons alive and doing well in Clarkstown. They should provide for her during her declining years.

Thus, on February 12, 1795, five Clarkstown residents found themselves called before the justices of the peace at the Court of General Sessions in New City. Isaac, John, Abraham, and Daniel Martine and William Felter were ordered immediately to "relieve and maintain the said Susanna Burray their said Grandmother with sufficient meat drink washing lodging & cloathing [sic]."[11]

---

(11) Case of Susanna Burray, "At a Court of General Sessions of the peace holden at the Court house in New City in and for the County of Orange on the twelfth day of February 1795," Budke Collection, BC-35.

There could be little doubt of the ability of the grandsons to support Susanna. The Martines had been prominent for several years, and William Felter also had a prosperous farm and home. Back in 1787 Daniel and John Martine and William Felter had been assessed by the Clarkstown tax assessor at £473, £271, and £196 respectively. [12] In addition, Daniel had six slaves back in 1790 and still owned at least four. William Felter had been looking around for a couple of slaves himself. [13] These were obviously men of means, well capable of providing for one elderly woman. Families should take care of their own. In this instance, the local overseers of the poor just wanted to make sure that they did so.

Rockland County's population in the 1790s was varied: rich and poor; farmers, millers, storekeepers, and day laborers; men and women in the prime of life, the elderly, and children; white families of English, Dutch, French, and German descent; Africans, both free and enslaved; and a few remaining Native Americans. This diverse population had spread out from the original Hudson River communities settled in the late 17th century. By the end of the 18th century there were four separate townships with widely scattered farms. Occasional hamlets had grown up around industrial centers, such as grist and saw mills, at crossroads, and at the social and religious centers near the county's five churches.

The population was not evenly distributed throughout the county. The rugged, mountainous terrain split off one section of the county from another, encouraging the growth of isolated farmsteads and hamlets. Entire areas of the county, particularly the rugged Ramapo and Haverstraw mountains to the west and north, were largely empty of human habitation. The few Indians, Ramapoughs, members of the Munsee group of the Lenape, or Delaware, generally made their homes back in the mountains, away from the white man. Other more fertile areas, with open valleys and flatlands, particularly in the center of the county around Hempstead and the older settlements along the Hudson, had more densely populated centers. Nor was the character of

---

(12)   "Clarkstown District Tax List for 1787."
(13)   In 1800 Martine would own four slaves and Felter would have two. "Federal Census 1800."

the population the same throughout the county. The longest settled area, Orangetown, displayed distinctly different population characteristics from the other three towns, especially Hempstead and Haverstraw, the two "frontier" areas of Rockland.

The description of Rockland County's population in the 1790s that follows is based on an analysis of the 1790 and 1800 federal census. The 1790 census for Orange County includes the townships of Orangetown and Haverstraw that would become the future Rockland County. This provides the base picture for the Rockland area in 1790. The 1800 census for Rockland County provides enumerations for the towns of Orangetown, Haverstraw, Clarkstown, and Hempstead (the latter two being carved out of Haverstraw in 1791). A comparison of the two census reports shows an area with slow population growth, especially when compared to other local areas, such as Westchester County across the Hudson. The heads of households were primarily of Dutch or English descent, with a smattering of German and French. But there was also a large contingent of Africans. These men and women are seldom identified by name or sex, but they were an integral part of life in late 18th-century Rockland.

ORANGETOWN
in the 1790s

Peter Taulman was pleased. It was official, he was now the chairman of the Orange Town Library. He and more than 20 of his neighbors had met early in the summer of 1796, intent on forming a library corporation. After all, there was no reason why Tappan's citizens should not have their own library. They should not have to go to New Jersey or over to New York City when they wanted to read. Instead, they would buy their own books and set up a library right here, in Tappan.

His neighbors, mostly from Orangetown but also some from Clarkstown and a few from Bergen, had raised over £40 for the proposed library. They had selected a board of trustees that June. Peter had been elected chairman. Simon Van Antwerp, Philip Dubey, Jacob Outwater, Samuel G. Verbryck, James Edwards, James Demarest, and Thomas Blanch, Jr., now served as the library's first board of trustees.[14] These were good men. Many had wealth and held positions of importance in the community. They should be able to choose the best books to fill the town's needs.

Samuel G. Verbryck's father had been the minister at Tappan and Clarkstown for years, dying right after the Revolution. Samuel had spoken about his plans to run for the state assembly at the next election. He could provide advice on political books that might be of interest. James Demarest, currently the town clerk for Orangetown, James Edwards, the county coroner, and Peter Taulman, himself a former assemblyman, all had experience with public affairs. They could be trusted to spend their neighbors' moneys wisely. They already had proved their ability to manage wealth. With the exception of Taulman, they all owned slaves. Verbryck had seven slaves and Edwards owned five. James Demarest may only have had two slaves, but he was still one of the wealthiest men in

---

(14)   "Incorporation of the Orange Town Library," June 14, 1796, *Historical Miscellanies*, I, p. 208.

town. That summer his tax appraisal totaled £935. James Edwards wasn't too far behind with an appraisal of £782, then came Samuel Verbryck with £584. Peter had been appraised at £369. Of course not everyone was that wealthy. Philip Dubey just made that year's assessment list, and he didn't even own any real estate, just £5 worth of personal property. Still, he could read and wanted to see the library become a reality.[15]

They wanted several different types of books — philosophical, inspirational, and practical. Books like Miller's *Gardener's Dictionary*, the *Encyclopedia or Universal Dictionary*, Buchan's *Domestic Medicine*, and *Agricultural Transactions* would provide basic information that could help around the farm and in the home. Historical works like Smith's *History of New York*, Brisson's *Narrative*, Anson's *Voyage*, and Voltaire's *History of Charles the XII* would make worthy additions. The spiritual needs of the community would also be taken care of. Edwards' *On Religious Affections*, Whitefield's *Sermons*, Fordyce's *Sermons*, *Letters from the Dead to the Living*, and works like *Practice of Piety* would help the library's members to understand their moral responsibilities. Other works like *The Spectator* provided commentary on daily happenings while *The Rudiments of Taste* might help improve manners. Some of the young men in the community really should read *Young Man's Companion* or Voltaire's *On Toleration*. Wives as well as husbands might be able to get more work out of the help if they had the pamphlet *Advice to Servants* readily available. *Wheatley's Poems* showed that the local community was well aware of this talented African slave who first published her poems in 1773.[16]

(15)   "Tax List for Orangetown, 1796," Budke Collection, BC-23.
(16)   "Catalogue of Books of the first Library in the town of Orangetown," 1805, Collections of The Historical Society of Rockland County.

These were only some of the books that the trustees
considered buying. It was exciting. All that knowledge
and thought would soon be available right here in Orangetown. All you had to do was be a member of the library
and whole new worlds could be yours.[17]

By the 1790s, Orangetown had enjoyed over a century of growth.
It was the smallest of the townships of Rockland, accounting for 13%
of the total acreage, or about 14,784 acres of land.[18] It was, however,
the most prosperous region in Rockland. Its residents were the wealthiest in the county. It had the strongest Dutch character, with a majority
of the families of Dutch ancestry. It also had a very prominent African
population. It was the most densely populated area. Its population was
also the oldest, and its growth rate was the fastest of any area in
Rockland at the end of the 18th century.

Changing Households

In 1790 Orangetown's population totaled 1,160 people in 190
households. By 1800 the population had increased to 1,332 in 221
households.[19] The population grew by nearly 15% during the last
decade of the 18th century. In the county as a whole, the population
increased by only 7%. The rate of growth in new households was
similarly higher in Orangetown. In the county as a whole the increase
in new households was only 11%, but Orangetown's households increased by 16%. This should not be interpreted to mean that only 31
new households formed. A comparison of the 1790 and 1800 census
reveals that only half of the heads of household on the 1790 census also
appeared on the 1800 census.

---

(17)   It isn't known how long the Orangetown Library remained active. A note in the cata-
       logue says that the library's books, numbering at least 342 volumes, were "divided up
       among the Members." This would have occurred early in the 19th century.
(18)   The acreage figure comes from Cole, *History of Rockland County*, p. 95.
(19)   The population figures used in the following pages do not always agree with the figures
       provided in the published versions of the 1790 and 1800 census for Rockland County.
       Each household was placed in a database and the numbers used are drawn from the data-
       base. In general, the discrepancies are small and do not have a significant impact on the
       overall picture of Rockland's population as it is presented in the following pages.

The composition of the existing households obviously underwent significant shifts throughout the 1790s. As expected, adult children left home, married, and started their own households. But these newly formed households could not account for the disappearance of 50% of the adult householders on the 1790 census. Eleven new widows appear on the 1800 census as heads of household, reflecting the deaths of a small proportion of the adult males by 1800. However, there certainly was no rash of deaths among adult householders in the 1790s that could account for the disappearance of 95 names from the census rolls in 1800. Instead, it seems probable that many of the older heads of households on the 1790 census stepped down to become members of a son's or daughter's household by 1800. The same household now appeared under the name of the son or son-in-law who had taken it over. It is also possible that some of the individuals migrated to New Jersey or north into Orange County. Some migration also would have occurred between Rockland towns.

The Orangetown households in 1790 varied in size from 1 to 16.[20] By 1800 the variation ranged from 1 to 20.[21] The more typical household fell in between, with an average household size of six persons. This household generally included the nuclear family of mother, father, and children. But it might also have other adult members, such as adult children who had not yet married, adult brothers or sisters who had not yet set up a separate household, or elderly parents or grandparents.

These variations in the size and composition of households held for all areas of Rockland County, but the households of Orangetown had several distinct traits that clearly differentiated this older, settled part of Rockland from the other areas. For one, Orangetown was the only area in which females comprised more than half the white population in both 1790 and 1800, with the percentage growing over the decade.[22] In the county as a whole, males accounted for 51.2% of the population.

---

(20)   In 1790 Jacob Gross and Dorothy Stevens had households of one; John DeWint and William Sickles had households of 16, including 7 slaves in each.

(21)   Darkes Ackerson, Maria Ternure, and James G. Blauvelt had single-person households. The Frederick Blauvelt household had 20 persons, including 9 slaves.

(22)   In 1790 white females accounted for 50.2% of the white population. By 1800, this increased to 51.6%.

Women as Heads of Households

As might be expected in a community with more females, Orangetown had the highest percentage of households headed by women. Female heads of households accounted for 6.4% of the white households in both 1790 and 1800. The 12 women listed on the 1790 census headed households that varied in size from 1 to 10. It appears that at least nine households included children under the age of 16. Most of these women were wealthy. Nine of the 12 either had high tax appraisals or owned slaves. Eleoner [sic] Ackerson (Eckerson) was appraised for £566 in 1796, while Catherine Blauvelt (called Catrina on the appraisal list) was appraised £466. Mary Blauvelt's property was appraised at £304, while Anna Briggs owed £0.3.8 in taxes on her £217 appraisal. Seven of the female households in 1790 included slaves, with anywhere from one to seven enslaved Africans in these households.[23] The three remaining female households, having far fewer resources, either had no appraisals or very low appraisals (Margaret Ackerson, £29) and owned no slaves (Hannah Blauvelt with a household of seven and Dorothy Stevens, who lived alone.)

While the 1790 female households appear to have been quite well-to-do, the women householders of 1800 fared less well. Only 3 of the 14 women owned slaves: Elizabeth Blauvelt (five slaves), Margaret Graham (two slaves), and Catharine Tallman (one slave). Only Margaret Graham (£572) and Catharine Tallman (£446) had high property appraisals in 1796. The remaining households either had very low valuations (Margaret Ackerson, £29 and Margaret Cooper, £27) or did not appear on the appraisal list.

An Older Population

Orangetown had a significantly older population than the other areas by 1800. The 1800 census enumerates the white population by sex and age. In Orangetown, 40% of that population was under 16, 40%

---

(23)   Elizabeth Blauvelt owned seven slaves; Mary Blauvelt, four; Catherine Blauvelt and Sarah Thurman, three each. Two slaves each lived in the households of Catherine Bogert and Helena Lawrence. Sarah Onderdunk owned one slave.

was age 16 to 45, and 20% was 45 or older. In the county as a whole, white children under 16 made up 43% of the population; adults 45 and older accounted for only 14% of the population. These figures refer solely to the white population and do not include Africans, who are enumerated *en masse* without differentiation by age or sex.

Africans, Free and Enslaved

Africans, both slave and free, made up a significant portion of the population of Orangetown. Nineteen percent of the 1790 population was African, a figure that grew to 22% in 1800. The overwhelming majority of these Africans were enslaved. Of 224 Africans on the 1790 census, only 26 were free (12%). Of these 26 free blacks, nine lived in six different white households. The remaining 17 free blacks lived in three African households: Jacob Cartright's household of seven, Samuel Freeman's household of three, and Job Long's household of seven.

By 1800, the number of free blacks in Orangetown had increased to 37, 13% of the African population. This did not signal an increase in the number of free African households however. There were still only three African heads of households in 1800, but the households had shrunk in size. Job Long's household now contained only four individuals. Samuel Freeman's household remained constant at three. Jacob Cartright's household of seven disappeared entirely from the Orangetown census, to be replaced by the Peter Fortune household that numbered two. The 17 Africans who had lived in independent households in 1790 were reduced to only nine by 1800.

Unlike the situation in 1790, by 1800 the majority of free blacks lived as part of a white household. Instead of the six white households with free blacks in 1790, there were now 25. Twenty-two of these households included a single free black, while three households included two free blacks. Nearly 80% (19 of 25) of these households included both slaves and free blacks, and in all cases the slaves in the household outnumbered the free Africans. It is apparent that increasing numbers of Rockland residents were freeing their slaves during the 1790s, but they were not being freed to set up their own independent households. Instead they remained with the white families and seldom

Bill of sale, "Negro boy Named Dick,"
Robbert Sickels and others to William Sickels, Jr., November 14, 1791.
Collections of The Historical Society of Rockland County.
Photo by Jeffrey Hunter.

had the opportunity to establish their own separate households and raise a family.

The increase in the number of free Africans in white households by 1800 reflected the growing awareness in Rockland that slavery was going to disappear in New York. By the end of the 18th century the state legislature had begun to pass a series of laws which would eventually lead to the emancipation of all African slaves resident in New York by July 4, 1827. As of 1799, all slave children born after July 4, 1799 were free. However, these children had to remain in their white master's household as servants until the age of 25 for females and 28 for males. The newly freed Africans were legally free, but not independent.[24]

As mentioned above, these free blacks represented only a fraction of the African presence in late 18th-century Rockland. While only 26 free blacks lived in Orangetown in 1790, there were 198 enslaved Africans living in 78 white households. By 1800 the number of enslaved Africans had increased to 256, living in 92 households. More than two-fifths of the households in Orangetown included Africans.

As would be expected, the majority of householders had only one or two slaves. In 1790, 26 householders owned a single slave while an additional 24 households included two slaves. By 1800 the number of households with a single slave had increased to 32, but households with two slaves decreased to 19. Households with large numbers of slaves occupied the other end of the spectrum. In 1790 five households owned seven Africans; one resident owned nine.[25] In 1800 five households included seven or more slaves.[26]

There was an obvious link between slave ownership and wealth. Although the attitude is difficult to understand and cannot be condoned, with few exceptions 18th-century New Yorkers overwhelmingly viewed African slaves as chattels, personal property, not as people. In a legal and economic sense, they were one of the most valuable types of livestock and were listed as such on inventories and assessed as such by the local tax assessor. Ownership of another human being required a significant economic investment, and slave owners generally be-

(24) See Edgar J. McManus, *A History of Negro Slavery in New York* (Syracuse, N.Y.: Syracuse University Press, 1966), chap. 9, for an overview of principal legislation leading to the eventual emancipation of New York's African slaves.

(25) Elizabeth Blauvelt, William Sickles, Cornelius Smith, Samuel Verbryck, and John DeWint each owned seven slaves. James J. Blauvelt owned nine.

(26) Abraham Blauvelt and John Perry owned seven Africans; Jacobus Blauvelt, eight; Frederick Blauvelt, nine; and Abraham Lent, ten.

longed among the wealthiest segment of the population,[27] though not all of Orangetown's wealthy residents owned slaves. Of the top 15 Orangetown taxpayers appearing on one or both of the census lists as well as the tax list, 14 owned slaves. Those 14 all owned multiple slaves, and in several instances they had free Africans in their households as well as slaves. These include: Frederick Blauvelt (nine slaves); Jacobus Blauvelt (eight slaves); Cornelius Smith, William Sickels, and Abraham Blauvelt (seven slaves); Robert Sickels (six slaves, one free black); Cornelius Blauvelt (five slaves); Isaac Haring and Isaac Perry (three slaves, one free black).

Wealth of Residents

Considering the fact that the Orangetown area was the first to be successfully settled and had the best access to the Hudson and the major markets in New York, it is not surprising that Orangetown residents were the wealthiest in the county. Tax assessment lists for the Clarkstown District (1787), Hempstead (1794), and Orangetown (1796) have survived. The assessments are based on tax rates for real and personal estates set by law for the entire state, ensuring a more equitable assessment of property throughout the state. The 1799 act set out the personal possessions, with valuations, that were taxable.

---

(27)   Bill of Sale, "Robbert" Sickels, Annetye Perry, John Ferdon to William Sickels, Jr., "Negro boy Named Dick About Eight Years," £30, November 14, 1791, Collections of The Historical Society of Rockland County. Bill of Sale, Peter Demarest to Isaac Smith, Negro boy Claus, about seven years, $87, March 17, 1801, Collections of The Historical Society of Rockland County. Bill of Sale, Archibald Cassiday to Abraham D. Herring, Negro girl named Jane, 16, $181.25, September 15, 1800, Collection of Melville Demarest, Nanuet, N.Y., as seen in Budke Collection, BC-76. Bill of Sale, Peter Bogert, Bergen County, N.J. to Gerret Smith, "Slave Named Will aged about twenty Eight years," £75, June 2, 1792, Budke Collection, BC-80.

Ox or bull, 4 yrs. and up	$15
Cow, 4 yrs. and up[28]	$10
Neat Cattle,[29] 3 yrs.	$6
Neat Cattle, 2 yrs.	$4
Horse or mare, 1 yr.	$8
Horse or mare, 2 yrs.	$15
Horse or mare, 3 yrs.	$20
Horse (except stallions) & mare, 4-8 yrs.	$30
Gelding or mare, 9-12 yrs.	$20
Gelding or mare, 13-16 yrs.	$8
Stallion, 4 yrs. and up	$300
Mule, 1 yr.	$8
Mule, 2 yrs.	$16
Mule, 3 yrs. and up	$25
All swine, more than 1 yr. [30]	$3
Coach[31]	$800
Chariot and post chaise[32]	$700
Phaeton[33] or coachee (steel springs)	$300
Every other 4-wheel pleasure carriage & every 2-wheel top carriage	$100
Every other 2-wheel pleasure carriage	$50
Brass or steel wheel clock	$40
Gold watch	$50
Other watches	$12
Every able-bodied slave (for life), 12-50 yrs.	$100
River sloops & vessels 30-60 tons burden	$500
River sloops & vessels above 60 tons	$750[34]

(28) Each taxpayer was allowed one milch cow for family use, nontaxable.
(29) Neat cattle: steers, cattle raised for meat or draft, rather than cows for milk.
(30) Each taxpayer had the first eight swine tax-free. All swine above the number eight were taxed.
(31) A large, closed, four-wheeled carriage.
(32) Open, four-wheeled pleasure carriage with top.
(33) A light, open, topless four-wheeled pleasure carriage with no side pieces in front of seats.
(34) "An Act for the assessment and collection of taxes," April 1, 1799, Chap. 72, 22nd Sess., *Laws of the State of New York*, 4:402-404.

This list, or one very similar, was the basis for the surviving appraisals made in Clarkstown, Hempstead, and Orangetown. Orangetown residents had far and away the most valuable estates, both in terms of land and personal property. The highest valuation on all these lists is £2,464 for Cornelius Cor[nelius] Smith of Orangetown in 1796. In fact, 19 taxpayers on the Orangetown list exceed the highest valuation found in either Clarkstown or Hempstead.[35] When examining comparable wealth among the various towns, Clarkstown residents have the second highest valuations, with Abraham Thew clearly the wealthiest Clarkstown inhabitant in 1787 (£785.10.0). Hempstead residents run a distant third, with John Suffern having property assessed at £544 in 1794.[36]

Dutch Predominance

The 1796 appraisal list and census lists also make it clear that a relatively small number of surnames dominated Orangetown, and most of them were of Dutch origin. Blauvelts abounded in Rockland, but they were concentrated in the southern portion of the county at the end of the 18th century. Thirty-four Blauvelt households appear on the 1790 Orangetown census, increasing to 37 in 1800. An additional 22 Blauvelt families lived in Haverstraw Township in 1790, with the overwhelming majority in the Clarkstown area.

On the 1790 census the Blauvelts of Orangetown are followed by numerous Smiths, Mabies, and Ackermans. These four surnames account for over 30% of the total households in Orangetown. If eight additional names are added: Bell, Bogert, Conklin, Hendrickson, Onderdunk, Perry, Sickels, and Tallman, these families accounted for over half of all the households in the township. As the decade progressed, however, the preponderance of these old, primarily Dutch families was challenged increasingly by new settlers as well as the death of some of the older family members. The same 12 surnames that accounted for

---

(35) These 19 refer to residents of Orangetown who appear on one or both of the 1790 and 1800 census lists as well as the 1796 tax list. Some individual taxpayers in Orangetown do not appear on either census. They may be nonresidents of Orangetown, or they may have moved into Orangetown after 1790 and left before 1800, or they may have died by 1800.

(36) "Old Tax Lists — Tax List of the Town of New Hempstead (now Ramapo Township, Rockland County, New York) for the Year 1794," *The Rockland Record*, III (1940), pp. 64-66. A nearly illegible manuscript copy of this tax list is in the Budke Collection, BC-80.

over half of the households in 1790 accounted for only 44% of the 1800 households.

This clear domination of a few old families is unique to Orangetown. Although the same family names appear throughout the rest of the county, they never overwhelmed an area to the same extent as they did Orangetown in the 18th century. Even in neighboring Clarkstown, which experienced the next greatest concentration of old-line Dutch families, the same 12 surnames accounted for only 21% of the households in 1800. The remaining townships of Rockland County, Haverstraw and Hempstead, included even fewer households with Dutch surnames. They represent the other end of the spectrum that characterized Rockland County's population at the end of the 18th century.

Looking south from Peekskill, the artist captured the rugged terrain of Haverstraw Township in northern Rockland County on the west bank of the Hudson River.
"View from Peaks Kill looking South...3 June 1779,"
sepia drawing by Archibald Robertson.
Spencer Collection, The New York Public Library.

TOWN OF HAVERSTRAW:
Rockland North of Orangetown in 1790

If Orangetown represented the wealthy establishment of prosperous Dutch farmers in Rockland, Haverstraw represented the frontier
community. Here the farms were more scattered and less refined, the
population was younger, poorer, lived in smaller households and included a much greater mix of English and French along with the early
Dutch families. It had far fewer slaves, fewer female households, and
was inundated with children.

The 1790 and 1800 census each list a town of Haverstraw, but
they cannot be directly compared. The 1790 Haverstraw census covered all the area of Rockland north and west of Orangetown. This area
became three separate towns in 1791: Haverstraw on the north, Clarkstown on the southeast, and Hempstead on the southwest. As a result
the analysis of Rockland outside of Orangetown is general for the 1790
period and specific by township for 1800.

One of the factors that characterized Orangetown was the rapid
growth in the number of households at the end of the 18th century. They
increased by 16% between 1790 and 1800. The northern and western
towns experienced much slower growth rates. The total number of
households outside of Orangetown grew by 82 to 892, or by 10%
between 1790 and 1800. The growth of population was even less
impressive, particularly when compared with Orangetown. Orangetown's population increased by 15% in the last decade of the 18th
century, but the population in the areas north and west of Rockland went
up only 5%.[37]

---

(37)   In this analysis of the changing population in Rockland outside of Orangetown, the 1790
Haverstraw census is compared directly with a compilation of the 1800 census material
for Clarkstown, Hempstead, and Haverstraw. Thus, the 1790 census for Haverstraw includes 810 households. In the 1800 census, Clarkstown has 327 households, Hempstead
has 337, and Haverstraw has 228, or a total of 892 for the same area covered by the 1790
census.

Female Heads of Households

As expected of a more remote area, the white males in Haver-straw in 1790 outnumbered the white females, comprising 51.7% of the population outside Orangetown. With fewer women, there are propor-tionally fewer female heads of households. Rockland County, outside of Orangetown, had 30 female heads of families in 1790, or 3.7% of all white households. This compared to the 6.4% of households in Orange-town. The female households in 1790 Orangetown were characterized by wealth, with a majority of the women either owning slaves or having high tax appraisals. A far different picture emerges of the female householder outside Orangetown. Fewer than one-third of the 30 women appeared on an appraisal list, two on the 1794 Hempstead list, and seven on the 1787 Clarkstown list, with a typical assessment of between £115 and £180.[38] While over half the Orangetown women owned slaves, only three of the Haverstraw women had slaves in their households: Martha Hay (five slaves in 1790, two in 1800), Mary Myers (one in 1790), and Jane Van Houten (one in 1790). Females generally had smaller households than their male counterparts, with the average woman's household numbering 4.5; the average household size for the entire population was 5.9.

Africans, Free and Enslaved

If women played a less conspicuous role in independent house-holds north and west of Orangetown, free Africans practically disap-peared. The three African households of Orangetown in 1790 accounted for only 1.6% of the total households, but all of Rockland north of Orangetown had only three African households in 1790, or just 0.4% of all households. Caesar Guy with a family of three, Phillip Guy with a family of seven, and Solomon Siscoe with a family of three all had independent households in 1790. None of them, however, still maintained households in Rockland by 1800. Solomon Siscoe does appear on the 1794 Hempstead assessment list, with an estate valued at £2, the smallest assessment on the entire list. Members of the Siscoe

---

(38)   Hempstead: Margaret Dusenberry, £74.15.0; Jane Van Houten, £489.5.0. Clarkstown:
       Cornelia Benson, £115.10.0; Charity [Geertri] Mannel, £147.0.0; Mary Myers, £128.0.0;
       Mary Onderdunk, £160.5.0; Delilah Smith, £90.5.0; Barbara Snyder, £180.5.0; and
       Bridget Vanderbelt, £185.15.0.

family will be settled in Skunk Hollow on the Palisades in northern
New Jersey by the 1840s, but it is not known whether they were related
to these early Rockland free Africans.[39]

Just as independent African households played a diminished role
in the settlement of Rockland north of Orangetown, free Africans living
in white households were also few and far between. Only three of the
white households outside of Orangetown included free blacks in 1790.
African slaves also formed a much smaller portion of the population.
While enslaved Africans accounted for 19% of the Orangetown population in 1790, they made up only 5% of the population outside
Orangetown. Two out of every five households in Orangetown included slaves. In the rest of Rockland only 14% of households, or just
over one in seven, included slaves. Frontier communities generally had
not yet accumulated enough wealth to enable the farmers to acquire
slaves. Instead they relied on large numbers of children as a principal
source of labor on the family homestead. The much higher proportion
of children living in households outside Orangetown, as shown in an
analysis of the population figures for the individual towns in 1800,
somewhat lessened the need for additional laborers.

Ethnic Diversity

The other characteristic of Orangetown, the overwhelming presence of a few families, generally of Dutch descent, became diffused
outside of Orangetown. While 12 family surnames accounted for more
than half the residents of Orangetown in 1790, there is no such domination in Haverstraw. The Blauvelts remained one of the most numerous families with 22 households, but the English Conklins outnumbered
them with 30 households and the Smiths (who could have been English
but primarily were Dutch) with 34 households. The 1790 census also
listed 12 Ackersons, 12 Allisons, 10 Babcocks, 10 Gurnees, 9 Coopers,
7 De Baunds or De Bonds, 10 Demarests, 13 Onderdunks, 9 Sarvants
or Servants, 9 Tallmans, and a multitude of other surnames covering a
variety of Dutch, English, Irish, French, Scottish, and German back-
grounds.

---

(39)   Joan H. Geismar, *The Archaeology of Social Disintegration in Skunk Hollow: A 19th-
Century Rural Black Community* (Studies in Historical Archaeology) (New York: Aca-
demic Press, 1982), p. 29.

By 1800, the federal census clarified the divergence between Orangetown and the other parts of Rockland. Rather than just one large township outside of Orangetown, there were now three. For the first time it is possible to see how the four townships of Rockland evolved in different ways. While Orangetown remained the most settled, sophisticated, and wealthiest part of Rockland, the other townships ranged from Orangetown's example on one end of the spectrum to the continued existence of frontier communities in the far northern and western range of the county.

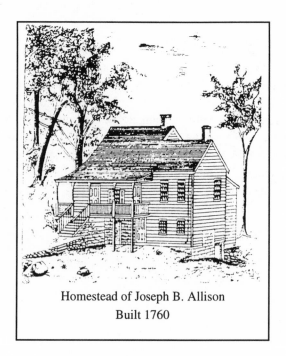

Homestead of Joseph B. Allison
Built 1760

Benjamin Allison House
Built 1754

The homes of Joseph B. Allison and Benjamin Allison
date from the mid-18th century.
These sketches, made in the mid-19th century,
include additions to the original houses.
From Cole, *History of Rockland County, New York.*

TOWN OF HAVERSTRAW
in 1800

The town had to be concerned about its reputation and Jacob Rose, Jr., was a definite cause for concern. The justices of the peace made sure that only the most reputable of men kept taverns, or inns, in Haverstraw, men who would ensure that their patrons behaved in a seemly and orderly manner. There was to be no cockfighting, gaming with cards or dice, billiard tables, or shuffle boards. Every one drank but not to excess. The tavern license clearly stated that disorderly behavior would not be tolerated, and the tavern keeper agreed to pay the town £50 in damages if he failed to keep an orderly house.[40]

Only men of the highest repute should keep taverns. Men like Andrew Suffern and David Burns understood how important it was to help Rockland grow. Andrew's father, John, was the county judge. Andrew had helped out at his father's store and tavern out at the crossroads leading to the Ramapo Pass. He knew how critical it was that travelers as well as the local farmers and laborers have a good place to meet, talk, exchange information, and get a good meal and a bed for the night when necessary. Now Andrew kept a store and tavern here in Haverstraw.

David Burns's father, Robert, had been the minister of the "English Church" over in Kakiat as well as at the Presbyterian church in Haverstraw. David and Andrew both served in the county militia. In fact, Andrew got his commission as an ensign in David's company back in 1792. David was the lieutenant colonel commanding the regiment.[41] Andrew was just starting out on his career, while David was already well established. He even had two slaves now to help him in the tavern and on the farm.

---

(40)   David Burns, Ebenezer Bishop, Tobias Derunde, Thomas North, Andrew Suffern, Joshua Taylor, Michael Trout, and Cornelius Waldron all received tavern licenses for the Town of Haverstraw in 1793-1794, Budke Collection, BC-35.

(41)   Commission to "Andrew Suffern, Gentleman," as "Ensign of a Company in the Regiment of Militia in the County of Orange whereof David Burns, Esq. is Lieutenant Colonel Commandant," April 19, 1792, Budke Collection, BC-80.

Jacob Rose, Jr., however, was a different man. He didn't seem to realize how important it was to help the community grow. He certainly didn't seem to have much of a stake in the community. He had a young family, four young sons, but he wasn't providing them with a good example. He was a common laborer, but many men started out that way and worked their way up to landowner and farmer. Instead, Jacob consorted with "evil" men and encouraged disreputable behavior. The drinking and carousing on New Year's Eve in 1799 might have been forgiven. People frequently got carried away at the end of the year, firing off guns in the night and generally making a nuisance of themselves. But that was five months ago and Rose continued to "keep and maintain a certain Common ill governed and disorderly house" where "certain evil and ill disposed persons of dishonest conversation" met both night and day, "drinking and tipling and misbehaving themselves."

If the community wanted to grow, to prosper, behavior like Jacob's had to be stopped. Maybe his indictment for keeping a disorderly house would make him reconsider the path he had chosen. Maybe he could become a productive member of the community once again. [42]

Men like Andrew Suffern and David Burns illustrate many of the characteristics that made Haverstraw so different from Orangetown. More than just Hook Mountain and geography separated the two areas. Orangetown continued to look to descendants of the original Dutch settlers for leadership in the community. Andrew, the son of an Irish immigrant who didn't arrive in Rockland until about 1770, and David, the son of a Scottish minister who didn't come to Rockland until 1760, belonged to the growing portion of the population with non-Dutch ancestry. They were the sons of relative newcomers, particularly when compared to the families in Orangetown, who had arrived in Rockland in the late 17th and early 18th centuries.

---

(42)   "The People of the State of New York & Jacob Rose, Jun., Indict. for keeping a disorderly house, May Term 1800," *Historical Miscellanies*, II, p. 233. Jacob Rose, Jr., pleaded not guilty to the charges. We do not know how this case was resolved.

A Frontier Community

Although Haverstraw was geographically larger than Orange-town, with 29, 572 acres of land,[43] it had the smallest population of any of the towns in Rockland in 1800, with only 1,253 people living in 228 households. Its households were the smallest in the county, averaging 5.5 people per household, compared to 6 persons in Orangetown. The small household size reflected significantly fewer older family members in the white population (only 14% versus 20% in Orange-town) as well as far fewer Africans (5% of the population versus 22% in Orangetown).

Smaller numbers of seniors and slaves were accompanied by a baby boom. While only 40% of Orangetown's white population in 1800 was under the age of 16, over half of Haverstraw's population (53%) were children, with 40% under the age of 10. The large numbers of children and relative absence of an older population are characteristic of a frontier community, one just opening up to young families. The absence of slaves is also a characteristic of the frontier. As seen in Orangetown, slave ownership corresponded strongly with wealth. Most people living on a frontier had not yet gathered enough surplus wealth to invest in slaves. They still needed the basics of life to survive on an isolated farmstead, the tools and equipment of agriculture necessary for the production of food and shelter for the family and their livestock. Labor could be provided by strong sons and daughters.

Africans, Free and Enslaved

The few Africans found in Haverstraw faced a far different environment than that experienced by their counterparts in Orange-town. There were only 65 Africans in the entire township, compared to the nearly 300 Africans who lived in the much more densely settled Orangetown. Fifty of these Africans were enslaved, the remaining 15 were free, but they all lived in white households. There were no free black households in this northern area of Rockland. The relatively small number of households with Africans — only 24 of the 228

---

(43) Cole, *History of Rockland County*, p. 95.

households in Haverstraw — meant that blacks were far more isolated from their fellows than in the more densely populated Orangetown. They had fewer opportunities to meet Africans from neighboring households and farms in the course of their daily work, meaning fewer opportunities to develop a sense of community amongst themselves. In Orangetown, proximity and greater numbers made it much easier for Africans to establish and maintain their own cultural norms, despite the fact that they lived almost exclusively in white households. They also had the example of free African households in the town. The Africans of Haverstraw weren't so fortunate.

Female Heads of Households

Households headed by females occupied a similar position in Haverstraw in 1800 as did their counterparts in Orangetown. There were 14 households headed by women in 1800, or 6.1% of all households. It appears that the number of female households was on the rise over the decade as the larger Haverstraw township of 1790 had only 3.7% of its households headed by women.

Wealth and Ethnic Diversity

There are no surviving assessment or tax lists for the town of Haverstraw, making it more difficult to establish the relative wealth of the residents. There was obviously some wealth, as indicated by the fact that over half of the slaves in Haverstraw lived in households with four or five slaves. Only well-established households could have supported this many slaves or have had sufficient work for four or more slaves. The men and women who owned slaves in Haverstraw were far more likely to be of English or French ancestry than Dutch. Of those residents who had three or more slaves in their household, John De Noyelles, Peter De Noyelles, and Isaac Gurnee were of French extraction; Robert Henry, Thomas Bryan, Eliza Smith, and Samuel Brewster were English; and Samuel Goetschius was Swiss. The wealth that had been concentrated in the hands of older Dutch families in Orangetown was dispersed among a variety of different national groups in the frontier area of Haverstraw.

The relative poverty of Haverstraw placed the community in a financial bind when it came to educating their children. In accordance with the 1795 law requiring each town to set aside tax dollars for the support of local schools, Haverstraw's "school moneys" were £19.10.0 in 1795, £12.15.3 in 1796, and £24.5.0 in 1797. These were the lowest assessments for school funds in all of Rockland's towns. This low assessment occurred at exactly the same time that Haverstraw's population included the highest proportion of children under the age of 16 in the county. Orangetown, with the fewest children of all the towns in Rockland, earmarked £32.0.0 in 1795, £25.10.0 in 1796, and £22.14.0 in 1797 for educational needs. This meant that Haverstraw had roughly 1s. 10d. to spend per child between 1795 and 1797, while Orangetown residents could spend 3s. 10d. on their children during the same period. During the same years, Clarkstown allocated approximately 3s. 2d. per child and Hempstead allocated 2s. 6d.[44] As frequently happens, the area most in need of educational services was least able to pay for them, even two hundred years ago.

---

(44) These figures are estimates since we do not know the number of children in each town in
      1795-1797. Instead, the number of children under 16 is taken from the 1800 census.
      This is divided into the total amount of money allocated for education by each town in
      1795-1797. The numbers are not exact, but they do allow us to see the relative spending
      in each of the townships. "Orange County, N.Y. Board of Supervisors Proceedings,
      1723-1798," Budke Collection, BC-9, pp. 347, 356, 366.

TOWN OF HEMPSTEAD
in 1800

As Lewis Shuart looked out his window at the
Ramapo River in July 1798, he had to wonder about just
what the dam and nail manufactory would really mean to
him and his neighbors. Things had not been the same
since John Suffern sold that 119 acres of land three years
ago. Everything used to be farmland and wood lots. Now
J.G. Pierson & Brothers had opened the sluicegate for the
first time. Their rolling mill, slitting mill, and nail factory
were up and running.

John Suffern

John Suffern settled in New Antrim (Suffern) in the Ramapo
Valley in the 1700s and became one of the most prominent
citizens of the Town of Hempstead (Ramapo). Silhouette,
probably early 19th century.
From *The Rockland Record*, III (1940).

Lewis had profited from the venture. When Josiah and Jeremiah Pierson first arrived in May 1795, he had met with them and agreed to house some of their workmen. There had been tenants farming the land for Suffern, but the Piersons had no use for farms. They needed men to build a dam, clear the land, raise the factory, prepare the machinery, and do a thousand other tasks. The tenant farmers had to get off the land immediately, but Josiah promised them work if they wanted to stay to help build his nail manufactory, which would be powered by the Ramapo River.[45] That first summer Lewis, along with neighbors John Smith and the Widow Van Blarcum, housed and fed 75 men, 20 carpenters and 55 common laborers. Just that first summer the Piersons had to do so much hauling and loading that they kept six teams of oxen busy. The work stopped in late October before the winter closed in, but Lewis and his neighbors had all profited from the new enterprise.[46]

Josiah Pierson had returned quickly to New York City to oversee their nail works there, but Jeremiah spent as much time as possible in the Clove, overseeing the work and making sure it progressed smoothly. He spent a lot of time traveling by stage up and down the Albany Road, checking on the work in Ramapo, then returning to his family in New York City. He, his wife Sarah, and their baby daughter Elizabeth finally moved to the Ramapo Works in June of 1796.

The nail manufactory had been Josiah Pierson's dream, but as time passed they saw less and less of Josiah. During the first two summers he had come up frequently, consulting with Jeremiah on all aspects of the work. Then, last summer and fall his visits were constantly delayed until they stopped entirely. They now knew that Josiah had been ill, suffering from consumption. He had died December 17, 1797 before his factory could be completed. Jeremiah Pierson and his younger brother Isaac now owned the nail works. Jeremiah looked as if he were

(45) Cole, *History of Rockland County*, p. 273.
(46) Josiah G. Pierson to Jeremiah H. Pierson, October 30, 1795, in Edward Franklin Pierson, "The Ramapo Pass," unpublished manuscript, 1915, ed. H. Pierson Mapes, 1955, p. 116.

going to stay in Ramapo, letting Isaac handle the business affairs from the New York City office.

Now the factory was in full operation. That spring Lewis watched as the workmen unloaded and installed 31 heading machines and 65 hammer and nail cutting machines. Isaac Pierson had shipped them up from their nail manufactory on Marketfield Street in New York City, closing down their New York City factory and consolidating all their industrial operations on the Ramapo. The J.G. Pierson & Brothers business operation, however, remained in the city.[47] The carpenters and laborers needed to build the works had gone, but they had been replaced by the nail and hoop makers. Nearly 20 of them now lived at the works.[48]

Jeremiah had told him that they made machine-cut nails, using a machine patented by Josiah, the first of its kind to give satisfactory results. The factory also cut hoops for barrels, primarily for the whaling industry. The cutting machines at the works could cut hoops in widths ranging from one-and-an-eighth inch to three inches.[49]

Now Lewis Shuart, the Piersons, and all the neighborhood would wait to see if the new venture could be a success. Many wondered whether it could possibly prosper since much of the iron for the mills had to be shipped in from Russia, then carried overland on pack trains from either Haverstraw or from Hackensack, New Jersey. The finished nails and hoops had to be carried, again by pack train, back to the Hudson at Haverstraw or to Hackensack and then shipped to New York. The transportation costs were high. The key to the Ramapo Works' continued success might ultimately lie in the development of a better, shorter land route to the Hudson, possibly through Nyack. But right now it did not exist.

---

(47)   Pierson, "The Ramapo Pass," p. 123.
(48)   The 1800 census shows that Jeremiah Pierson's household included 19 males age 16-25 and 6 males age 26-44. With the exception of Pierson himself, these 25 men undoubtedly worked at the Ramapo Works.
(49)   Josiah G. Pierson to Jeremiah H. Pierson, April 7, 1797, as quoted in Pierson, "The Ramapo Pass," p. 120.

The people of Hempstead more closely resembled their neighbors in Haverstraw than their neighbors to the east in Clarkstown and Orangetown. Like Haverstraw, Hempstead remained in many ways a frontier area of Rockland. The Ramapo Mountains pretty well made up half the township, and the terrain, particularly in the western and northern portions of the township, was generally unsuitable for farming. The largest of the four townships in Rockland, Hempstead included 44,783 acres.[50] Despite the relative inaccessibility of the area and the poor quality of the soil, Hempstead had the largest population (1,991) and the most households (337) in 1800. These households were quite similar to the Haverstraw households, although they were slightly larger, with an average of 5.9 persons per household, rather than 5.5. In size, at least, they more closely resembled the larger households of Orangetown.

Indians of Rockland

The population of Hempstead was overwhelmingly white. Africans accounted for just 5% of the population. The census reports of 1790 and 1800 specifically excluded Indians from the population enumeration, making it impossible to know how many Native Americans remained within Rockland County's borders at the end of the century. If they did, they undoubtedly lived in the Ramapo Mountains along the Rockland County, New York-Bergen County, New Jersey border. White settlers in the area claimed that the last of the Native Americans departed from the Ramapo Pass in 1747, moving westward to join other members of the Lenape/Delaware tribe.[51] Continued references to Native Americans in this area, the "Jackson Whites" of the 19th and 20th centuries, suggests that at least a few tribal members

---

(50)   Cole, *History of Rockland County*, p. 95.
(51)   Cole relates the story of Elizabeth Eisler, born 1740, who said that in 1747 the Indians of the area gathered near her father's house north of New Antrim and departed the area, never to return. *History of Rockland County*, p. 263.

from the original Munsee, or Ramapough, remained.[52] It is likely that these remaining Native Americans passed freely back and forth between Rockland and Bergen counties. It is impossible, at this late date, to establish a specific residence, especially as the Ramapough had both summer and winter camps.[53]

A Young, Productive Population

The white population was young, nearly as young as that in Haverstraw. Almost 50% of the population was under the age of 16. There was, however, one important difference: the Hempstead population included far more adolescents and pre-adolescents aged 10 to 16. These youngsters accounted for 16% of the white population, rather than the 13% seen in Haverstraw. The presence of a large number of older children meant that the families could be more productive than their counterparts in Haverstraw. Children from age 10 to 16 performed all kinds of work around the farm and in the house, work that was too hard or too dangerous for their younger siblings. This enabled the farmers of Hempstead to be more productive, with more successful farms and a greater accumulation of wealth than in Haverstraw.

The Hempstead population also included relatively few older family members, defined by the census as 45 and above. Fourteen percent of the white population was age 45 and older, a figure identical to that for Haverstraw. Next to young children, these individuals were the least productive group in the population. Their small number is consistent with the frontier status of Hempstead. Young, productive households dominate frontier areas.

---

(52) Report of Roger D. Joslyn, C.G., F.A.S.G., on the genealogy of the Ramapough Mountain Indian tribe indicates that several different families were in the Ramapo Mountains at the end of the 18th century, but it is unclear whether they lived in New York or New Jersey. Albert J. Catalano and Ronald J. Jarvis, "Response to Proposed Findings" before the Department of the Interior, Washington, D.C., "In the Matter of the Petition of the Ramapough Mountain Indian Tribe for Federal Acknowledgement as an Indian Tribe," May 8, 1995.

(53) Telephone conversation between Ralph Sessions and Jacquetta Haley, November 8, 1995; telephone conversation between Albert J. Catalano and Jacquetta Haley, November 8, 1995.

Africans, Free and Enslaved

The relative dearth of slaves is another indication of the frontier status of this township. The town's 100 African residents included six free blacks, all living in white households, and 94 slaves. The 56 slaveowners comprised 17% of the town's households. These 56 townsmen and women differed dramatically from their counterparts in Haverstraw because the slaves were far more evenly distributed among the households rather than concentrated in a few hands. Here, 66% of the slaves lived in households with only one or two slaves. In Haverstraw more than half the slaves lived in households with four or five slaves. Slave ownership still implied above-average wealth, but it does not seem to have meant a few individuals with large concentrations of wealth as it had in Haverstraw.

Distribution of Wealth

The 1794 Hempstead tax list provides some indication of how wealth was distributed among the town's population. As in Orangetown in 1796, not all wealthy people owned slaves, but the overwhelming majority of those residents with high property assessments also owned slaves. Of the men and women with the top 15 assessments, varying from £544.0.0 for John Suffern to £252.5.0 for Gilbert Johnson, 11 owned slaves in 1790 or 1800.[54] Although John Suffern and John Gurnee each had four slaves in their households in 1800 and John D. Coe owned six, the remaining eight leaders on the assessment list had just one or two enslaved Africans in their households.[55] Out of the next 15 top tax assessments, only seven included slaves in their households in 1790 or 1800.

The few free blacks residing in Hempstead lived in white households with slaves. Of the six households with free blacks in 1800, five

---

(54)   These top 15 include only those individuals who also appear on either the 1790 or 1800 census.

(55)   Aaron Blauvelt, two slaves, 1790; Jane Van Houten, one, 1790; Abraham Herring, one slave in 1790, two in 1800; Matthias Barbaro, one slave, 1800; James Van Buskirk, one, 1790; Herman Blauvelt, two, 1800; Andrew Van Orden, one, 1790; Stephen Gurnee, one slave in 1790, two in 1800.

had both free and enslaved Africans: John Gurnee (one free, four slaves), John D. Coe (one free, six slaves), Gilbert F. Cooper (one free, five slaves), John Quackenbush (one free, two slaves), and Henry Derunde (one free, one slave). Abby Gurnee was the only Hempstead resident to have a free African as part of her household without owning additional slaves. A widow with five children under the age of 10, three boys and two girls, Abby undoubtedly could use all the help she could get, both in the home and on the farm.

Female Heads of Households

Abby was one of just 19 women who headed households in 1800 Hempstead. These women accounted for 5.6% of the households, the lowest of any town in Rockland. Like the women of Haverstraw, there is little to indicate that they were nearly as well-off as the widows of Orangetown. Clausy Smith, an elderly woman, had a household of two, herself and a slave; Abby Gurnee, as mentioned above, had a free African in her household, probably a former slave. Four of the women on the 1800 census appear on the 1794 Hempstead tax list, but their assessments are generally modest. The Widow Deronde (Catherine) was appraised for £135.9.0, Margaret Dusenberry for £74.15.0, Margaret Gurnee for £23.0.0, and Elizabeth Wanamaker for £78.0.0. The remaining female heads of households did not have estates large enough to be assessed in 1794. By way of comparison, John Suffern's assessment of £544.0.0 was the highest in the town. The four women on the 1794 assessment list certainly were not impoverished, but they had much less property than their male counterparts.

Ethnic Diversity

The variety of surnames on the tax rolls and the census reports indicates that Hempstead, again like Haverstraw, had a far more diverse population than Orangetown. The name Hempstead came to Rockland County with a group of English settlers from Hempstead, Long Island, who arrived in then Orange County in the 1720s. These early English settlers and their descendants were joined by French Huguenots, Germans, Irish, and Scottish, as well as settlers of Dutch descent crossing over from nearby Bergen County or moving out from Orangetown. In 1800 there were 19 Conklin households, 17 Smiths, 13 Gurnees, 9 Ackersons, 7 Debauns plus 6 Quackenbushes and 6 Wanamakers. Otherwise there were seldom more than three or four households with the same surname. No single family dominated Hempstead in the way the Blauvelts seemed to permeate every part of Orangetown.

TOWN OF CLARKSTOWN
in 1800

Every year they faced the same problem: How would the town pay for the needs of the poor and the homeless? Moneys from taxes just never went far enough. And what did you do with people who had nowhere to live, let alone money for food or clothing? The town accepted its responsibility for these people, but the tax dollars just never went far enough. Clarkstown's overseers of the poor in 1795, Aurt Polhemus and Evert Hogenkamp, would use the same methods their predecessors had been using for years: sell the services of the able-bodied poor so that the town had enough funds to take care of the children and the helpless.

Several of Clarkstown's most prominent citizens arrived at the courthouse on April 11 for the yearly sale of the poor. If you could not afford a slave but needed additional hands to help out on the farm or in the mill or around the house, the overseers of the poor usually could solve your problem. Today there were nine able-bodied poor offered for sale, four men and five women.

Daniel Blauvelt could certainly use a helping hand around the farm. There were four women at home, including two girls, but he had only one young son to help on the farm. Jeremiah Yeomans was in his prime and so he should be able to do a lot of the daily farm chores. He would be worth the £12.9.0 that the overseers charged for a year's service, especially as the town was willing to pay for his clothing needs during the year. Isaac Blauvelt paid £10 for Mary Bayard for a year, and she would provide her own clothing. His wife would undoubtedly welcome

some help in the house, garden, and dairy. Jacobus Blauvelt paid £9 for Phebe Brewer for the next year. She
wasn't quite as expensive as Mary, but Jacobus had to
provide for all her clothing needs.

The other indigents did not look as capable. Edward
Smith paid £7 to the town for Paul Metsher, and Daniel
Van Sickles paid £9 for Isaac Felter, but the overseers
provided clothing in both cases. The other women, perhaps girls, had fewer skills. Isaac Smith took Ann Jones
for £4, while Abraham Jersey paid only £3 for Elizabeth
Brewer. Rachel Jones might be a little more productive.
Daniel Van Sickles was willing to pay £5 for a year of her
service.

Harmanus Perry must have really wanted Peter Hoffman. He paid £35 for a year's service. Admittedly Perry
had a young family. There were just he, his wife, and their
sons and daughters all under the age of 10. But that was
a lot of money for one man's labor. Perry had better hope
that Hoffman really did have some special skills that
would make him worth the extra money.

By the end of the day, Aurt Polhemus and Evert
Hogenkamp could be pleased with the addition to the
coffers for the poor. The sale of these nine indigents
brought in £94.9.0 for the town.[56]

If Hempstead's population was like that of Haverstraw and the
frontier, Clarkstown's residents more closely resembled those of
Orangetown. Proximity to the Hudson River, the 18th century's greatest highway in New York, and to Orangetown easily explains the
similarities. The residents of Orangetown moved outward as the population grew. Some moved westward into Bergen County, New Jersey,
where many of the old Dutch families remained strong. These former
Rockland residents are outside the scope of this study. Others, however, moved northward into Clarkstown. Thus Clarkstown, which

(56) "Clarkstown, N.Y. Supervisors of the Poor, Account Book, 1793-1819; 1846-1867,"
      Budke Collection, BC-7. The account book shows £93.9.0 as the total received from the
      sale, but the individual amounts add up to £94.9.0

contained the county seat at New City after 1774, included a much higher concentration of Dutch families, had older families, had more households with Africans, either slave or free, had a higher rate of wealth, and generally enjoyed greater prosperity than either Hempstead to the west or Haverstraw to the north.

In area, Clarkstown included only 22,693 acres,[57] making it the second smallest township; yet its population in 1800 was 1,811 in 327 households, second only to Hempstead. There were no major population centers. Even New City, site of the courthouse, was little more than a crossroads. In general, Clarkstown, like Hempstead and Haverstraw, consisted almost entirely of scattered farmsteads rather than settled hamlets, such as Tappan, Nyack, and the Slote in Orangetown.

In Clarkstown white males outnumbered females, 52% versus 48%. The households came closest to the Orangetown model, with 46% of the population under age 16 and a relatively large proportion of the residents aged 45 and above, 15%. Nearly 40% of the population was age 16 to 45, the prime childbearing ages for women and the most productive years for men. The population as a whole was more mature than that in either Haverstraw or Hempstead, but still had a more youthful character than Orangetown.

Africans, Free and Enslaved

Africans made up nearly 9% of Clarkstown's population. Again, the overwhelming majority were enslaved, but two black families maintained independent households. Claus (no surname) had five members to his household, and Dick Cook's household numbered four. Five other free Africans lived in white households. David Pye had one free black in his household of 11, which also included five slaves. Theodorus Brower had one free black in his household. Daniel Waring's household included two free Africans in addition to himself, his wife, and his two young daughters. Peter Demarest had one free African as well as one slave.

---

(57)   Cole, *History of Rockland County*, p. 95.

The overwhelming majority of Africans, however, remained enslaved. The 1800 census included 149 slaves in 66 households. Half those Africans lived in households with three or fewer slaves. One in every five households in Clarkstown contained Africans, making it a distant second to Orangetown (two in every five households) in terms of the frequency with which Africans would be encountered in everyday life.

Distribution of Wealth

The greater number of slaves corresponds with the increased wealth of the residents of Clarkstown. Of the 15 residents with the highest assessments on the Clarkstown assessment list of 1787 — ranging from £785.10.0 to £276.5.0 — 13 owned slaves in either 1790 or 1800. Abraham Thew, the man with the highest assessment in Clarkstown in 1787 (£785.10.0) listed ten slaves in his 1790 household, a number that dropped to seven in 1800. Other principal slave owners included Daniel Martine with six slaves in 1790 and four slaves in 1800 (assessment £473.0.0), Theodorus Snedeker with six slaves in 1790 and four slaves in 1800 (assessment £418.5.0), and Major John Smith with four slaves in 1790 and five slaves in 1800 (assessment, £383.15.0). There were no women among the 15 inhabitants with the highest taxes.

Female Heads of Households

Although none of them topped the assessment roles, 22 women in Clarkstown were the heads of their households in 1800. They appear to have been slightly better off than the widows or female heads of households of Haverstraw and Hempstead. Seven of the 22, more than a quarter of these women, either owned slaves or appeared on the 1787 tax list. Four who are on the tax list had appraisals between £115 and £182, indicating that they owned substantial properties even though they weren't among the town's wealthiest individuals.[58] In addition

---

(58) Cornelia Benson, £115.10.0; Charity (Geertri) Mannel, £147.0.0; Mary Myers, £128.0.0; and Barbara Snyder, £180.5.0. Mary Myers listed one slave in her 1790 household, but held no slaves in 1800.

to these four women, two others owned slaves. In 1800 Catherine De
Vries had two slaves in her household of six, and Hannah Smith had
one slave in her family of six.

Ethnic Diversity

Families of Dutch ancestry in Orangetown had moved freely into
Clarkstown, but they never dominated this larger area as they had
dominated Orangetown. The Blauvelts seemed to be ubiquitous, with
20 households in Clarkstown, but the Smith households outnumbered
them by four. The Smiths could be either English or Dutch. Other
Dutch families thrived: there were 10 Vanderbilt households, 10 Tallman (Taulman), 8 Van Houten and Onderdunk, and 7 Van Orden.
There were also 7 Demarest households, 5 Sarvent (Servant), 6 Ackerson, 4 Campbell, and 3 Perry and Ternure. The 63 Dutch families
certainly did not constitute a majority of the households in Clarkstown
in 1800. Although they held important positions within the community,
they shared the power and wealth with various other nationalities,
especially the English and the French.

Chapter 5

❧

Preparing for
a New Century

Every decade can be seen as both a continuation of earlier events and a harbinger of things to come. It contains the elements of tradition — those ideas and ways of doing things that have been carried over from earlier times. It also contains the seeds of change — the emergence of those individuals who will shift the old ways in new directions and the gradual introduction of new ideas and technologies. Rockland County in the 1790s displayed just such a duality. The older, traditional ways appeared firmly in place, yet there were hints of possible changes.

Rockland residents led lives very similar to those of their fathers and grandfathers. They were farmers first and foremost. Their livelihood came from the crops they raised in their fields and gardens, the livestock that foraged through meadows and pastures, and the firewood and lumber in nearby wood lots. From these sources came their food, light for their homes, and heat for their hearths, even some of the cloth which kept them warm in winter.

They did not need to be totally self-sufficient. Proximity to the Hudson River meant that Rockland residents had access to the textiles and manufactured goods available in New York City. Small general stores in Tappan, Nyack, New Antrim, and Haverstraw provided local residents with a combination of dry goods, hardware, and miscellaneous goods that supplemented local production. Those Rockland residents furthest from the river had fewer opportunities to acquire these goods, but they were available.

Industries generally supplemented agriculture. Saw mills served the local communities, providing lumber for neighboring homes and barns. Grist mills ground the farmer's wheat, corn, and rye into flour and meal. Most of the flour and meal was returned to the farm for local consumption, with the excess barreled up and shipped off to the New York City market.

The newly constructed J.G. Pierson & Brothers nail manufactory was a different story. It was not an adjunct to the local agrarian economy. The men on the heading machines, the nail cutters, and the hammermen worked year-round. They did not work part-time on the local farms and part-time at the factory, according to the season. The output of the factory had an international market. The local farm community might purchase a small quantity of nails or barrel hoops, but the real market for the Piersons was New York City, the West Indies sugar plantations, and the whaling industry. The factory utilized waterpower of the Ramapo to power its mills, and wood from the rugged mountainsides to make charcoal to fire the iron furnaces. The natural resources which drew the nail manufactory to Rockland had little appeal for the broader, agrarian-based economy.

In this sense, the nail manufactory pointed toward the industries that would develop in Rockland in the first half of the 19th century. The quarries of Nyack and scattered brickyards along the Hudson existed in the 18th century, but they were small, local industries. They provided building material for their neighbors. In the 19th century both quarrying and brickmaking would serve the New York City market, providing building material for the rapidly expanding nation. They were extractive industries, making use of natural resources that were unimportant to the county's farming population. Special skills were required, although general laborers were also an important part of their labor force. The iron industry, the quarries, and the brickyards all represented the broadening of Rockland's economic base in the 19th century, an aspect of economic life that had just begun to appear in the 1790s.

The industrial growth hinted at by the opening of J.G. Pierson & Brothers in 1798 would ultimately rest on the development of new transportation routes. The Orange Turnpike, the first private turnpike company established in the state, represented a new attitude toward travel and transportation in New York. The geographic expansion of the state was accompanied by an expanded vision of the role of private enterprise in ensuring that all areas of the state would be accessible to people and commerce.

As the 19th century opened, the state promoted the private development of new transportation routes and technologies through grants of monopoly rights to groups of individuals willing to invest in the construction and maintenance of roads, canals, and other projects. The Orange Turnpike, passing through the western tip of Rockland County, was just the first of these endeavors that eventually resulted in such diverse projects as the Erie Canal in upstate New York and Fulton's steamboats on the Hudson River. In Rockland itself, the first quarter of the 19th century would see repeated efforts to construct a turnpike between New Antrim and Nyack. Such a route promised to shorten significantly the distance between the growing industries of the Ramapo Valley and the Hudson River. In turn, this would cut transportation costs dramatically and result in greater profits for the iron and textile industries that developed along the Ramapo River in Hempstead during the early 19th century.

The traditional methods of road construction and repair, relying on a maximum levy of 30 days' road work annually from the county's residents, remained in place well into the 19th century.[1] Increased road usage as the population and commerce expanded into new areas of New York proved too much for these old practices. The private turnpikes seemed to promise an alternative to meet the needs of the expanding nation without requiring increased tax dollars or higher labor levies for road maintenance.

By the 1790s the state was also showing a distinct interest in the education of its citizens. The education of children had long been a family matter. Parents decided whether their children would be educated and what they would learn. Generally, the settlers in a neighborhood would agree to hire a schoolmaster for their children and would pay him a set rate per child. If there were not enough families in an area to support a school, the parents could teach their children at home, send their children to relatives who lived near a school, or apprentice their son or daughter in a trade. Part of the apprenticeship generally included learning to read and write.

As the 19th century dawned, the nation's political leaders were increasingly aware that the success of the new American republic would rest on a well-informed, educated populace. New York State's leaders recognized this political fact when they voted to provide public support for education with the 1795 "Act for the encouragement of schools." For the first time state funds would be allocated for the education of children at the local level. At the same time the state required that the

---

(1)   The number of days' labor was raised from a maximum of 20 to 30 in 1797. "An Act to regulate highways," March 21, 1797, *Laws of the State of New York*, 4:53.

towns similarly provide local tax revenues for schools. The parents continued to decide if and when their children would attend school, but the town and state now agreed to pay some of the expense for educating the county's future voting citizens. The establishment of a public system of education occurred later in the 19th century, but its roots can be found in the 1790s.

The 1790s also displayed a gradual shifting in the population of Rockland County. Throughout the 18th century residents of Dutch ancestry had dominated the local political and economic scene. These were the descendants of the original settlers, especially in the Orangetown area. But they had been joined by Englishmen, Scots, Germans, Frenchmen, and other European settlers. In addition, the more prosperous residents brought in African slaves, adding another dimension to the population mix.

By the end of the 18th century this population mix was shifting away from the earlier Dutch dominance to a greater diversity and greater prominence for the non-Dutch residents of the county. The Dutch would continue to dominate the area around Orangetown, but in other parts of the county the Dutch were becoming a minority. During the early 19th century the traditional Dutch culture would remain strong, as indicated by the continued use of Dutch in the Dutch Reformed Church, but English was becoming the language of Rockland, just as it was the language of the rest of the state.

While the Dutch remained an important, if declining, part of the Rockland population at the end of the century, the fate of another major segment was much more troublesome. African-Americans increased as a proportion of the total Rockland population during the 1790s, going from 8% in 1790 to almost 10% in 1800. During this same period, the percentage of free Africans also increased slightly. But the passage of gradual emancipation laws in 1799 raised major questions relating to the future of all African-Americans in Rockland. As it became obvious that all New York slaves would eventually be freed, questions arose as to how they would fit into the broader white society. The decline in the number of free blacks living in African-American households in the 1790s, despite the rising number of free blacks, did not bode well for independent Africans in Rockland. Increasingly, free Africans remained in white households.

This probably reflected two factors. Increasingly white masters manumitted their African-American slaves while requiring that they continue to work for them for a set number of years. The price of emancipation was continued labor. Secondly, the surrounding white community had already taken the most productive lands and jobs. Freed African-Americans would have to go to areas of Rockland and neighboring New Jersey that the majority white population had already rejected as unproductive. The development of separate African communities in the early 19th century, such as that at Skunk Hollow on the Palisades, showed the tendency to push the independent African population into marginal areas. The growth of the African population in rural regions like Rockland would be severely limited in the early 19th century by this tendency to limit them to marginal areas. Many freed Africans would leave Rockland during the 19th century, seeking a more congenial lifestyle in urban areas such as New York City. Although these African-Americans continued to be relegated to the lowest paying jobs and the poorest sections of the city, the large numbers of Africans allowed them to build self-sustaining communities where their own culture and heritage would be revered, rather than reviled as it was by the larger white population.

While the African-American population began to cope with the promise of emancipation at the end of the 18th century, Native Americans in Rockland remained almost totally outside the day-to-day experiences of Rockland County's white residents. Nominally, the Ramapough had been excluded geographically since the middle of the 18th century. Today, it is almost impossible to identify specific Native American individuals or communities in Rockland in the 1790s. But their reemergence with a separate, distinct identity as part of the "Jackson Whites" in the 19th century points to their continued presence on the fringes of their former homeland. Late 18th-century Rockland County residents tended to ignore the Ramapough. Native American peoples were an element of the past that the European settlers in Rockland had physically and culturally removed. The perseverance of the Ramapough in the area, revealed by their reemergence in the 19th century as a separate mountain community, shows that the Ramapough had withdrawn from white contact but they had not vanished.

Any effort to gain a real understanding of life in Rockland County at the end of the 18th century must come from a sense of it as a dynamic community, not as a static picture. Like us, the residents of Rockland in 1798 looked back to earlier times while wondering what the future would bring. The creation of Rockland as a separate county in 1798 meant that its future would develop along lines separate from its northern and western neighbors in Orange County. The divisive geography that played a critical role in establishing the need for a separate jurisdiction "South of the Mountains" continued to be a crucial factor in the slow development of a better transportation network in Rockland County. But the transportation network was changing, and the population was expanding into areas that had been inaccessible earlier in the 18th century. This process would continue, gaining momentum in the first half of the 19th century as new technologies — the steamboat and the railroad — transformed the movement of goods and people.

Index

Coe, D. 80
Coe, John D. 133
   slaves 132
Coleman's boat 33
Colwill, Joshua 28
Conklin, Hannah 50
Conklin, John 96
Conklin families 114, 118,
   133
Constant, Rev. Silas 41, 80
Cook, Dick 136
Cooper, Gilbert F.
   slaves 133
Cooper, Margaret 108
Cooper families 118
Corbett, Capt. John 9
corn (maize) 61
   husking 67
Corneilson, Mr. (of Nyack) 33
Corneilson, Dr. Abm 37
Corneilson, Michael, Jr. 58
Court of General Sessions 48,
   101
courts
   child support 50
   county court 1, 48
   Goshen 1, 48
   indigence 101
   murder cases 49
   New City 6, 48, 101
   Tappan 1, 6
Coventry, Alexander 54, 68, 87
Coventry, William 54
Crèvecoeur, J. Hector St. John de
   71
crops 43, 44, 56, 59, 96
   harvesting/preparation of 61,
   66
   in summer 56
Crouter, Mr. 47
currency 100
   decimal-based dollar 100
Curtis, Hones 48

D

De Clark, Jacob 89, 91
De Clark, Jacobus 89
de Miranda, Francisco 23, 78, 85
De Noyelles, John 2, 3, 4, 5, 125
   slaves 125
De Noyelles, Peter
   slaves 125
De Pew, Peter 97
De Vries, Catherine
   slaves 138
Deane, Samuel 41, 44, 88
Debaun, A. 47
Debaun, Abraham 47, 98
Debaun, Abram 47
DeBaun, DeBond (see Debaun)
Debaun families 118, 133
Delaware Indians 102, 130
Demarest, James 104
Demarest, Peter 98, 112, 136
Demarest families 118, 138
Deronde, Catherine (widow)
   property assessment 133
Derunde, Henry
   slave 133
Derunde, Tobias 122
DeWint, John 107
Dixon, Edward 68, 84
Dobbin, Anthony 20, 21
Dobbs' Ferry 28
drownings 29
Dubey, Philip 104
Dunderberg Mountain 28
Dunlap, William 54, 63
Dunlop, J.B. 30, 64
Dunscomb, John 49
Dusenberry, Margaret 117
   property assessment 133
Dutch predominance 54, 114,
   115, 138, 142
   Blauvelt 114
Dutchess County
   roads 16
dyeing of yarn and fabric 76

Rockland Baptist Church (Nanuet
   Grace Conservative Baptist
   Church) 53
Rockland County 7
   establishment of 7
   geography 8, 13
   origin of name 9
   population 102, 103
   South of the Mountains 1, 2
Rockland Lake (see Quaspeck
   Pond)
Rose, Jacob, Jr. 49, 122, 123

S

Sarvent, Philip 80
Sarvent (Servants) families 118,
   138
saw mills 40, 81, 96
School Act of 1795
   97, 146
schools (see education)
Schuyler, General 69
Secor, Jacob 99
sheep 73
   Cheviot breed 73
   environment 74
   predators of 74
Shuart, Lewis 127, 128, 129
Sickels, Robbert
   slaves 112
Sickels, William, Jr. 112
Sickels families 114
Sickles, William 107
   slaves 107, 111, 112
Siscoe, Solomon 117
Siscoe family 117
skating 86, 87
Skunk Hollow 117, 143
Slaughter's Landing 28
slavery 111
slaves (see also Africans) 45, 48,
   93, 95, 104, 108, 109, 112, 117,
   123, 124, 132, 133, 136, 138

African 142
Clarkstown 136, 137, 138
Claus (boy) 112
Cuff 54
Dick (boy) 112
emancipation laws of 1799
   109, 146
Haverstraw 117, 125
Hempstead 132, 133
Jane (girl) 112
Orangetown 108, 109, 117
Prince 49, 77
sale of 48
Tom (Tallman's) 93
Wheatley 105
Will (Smith's) 112
Will (Tallman's) 93
sledding 87
sleds 81, 84, 86
sleighs 23, 84
sloops 31, 32
Slote (ditch) 14
Slote (see Tappan Slote)
Slott, William 99
smallpox 37, 39
Smith, Adolphus 44
Smith, Alb't 47
Smith, Capt. 33
Smith, C. 47
Smith, Clausy 133
Smith, Cornelius
   slaves 111, 112
   wealth 114
Smith, Deliah 117
Smith, E. 80
Smith, Edward 135
Smith, Eliza
   slaves 125
Smith, Garret 47
Smith, Gerret 112
Smith, Hannah
   slaves 138
Smith, Isaac 112, 135
Smith, John 128